Career Coach GPT:

The Complete Guide to ChatGPT Resume, Cover Letter, Interview, and Job Search Success

Jeremy Schifeling

CONTENTS

Introduction: Career Coaching for All

What's the hardest part of the modern job search?

It's not resumes.

It's not LinkedIn.

It's not even interviewing.

It's the fact that you have to navigate all these obstacles *alone*.

And so even the best job-seekers often give up or settle for a mediocre job - just so they can end the lonely misery.

Not only have I been there myself as a former kindergarten teacher trying to make the leap to Silicon Valley, but I've seen it thousands of times as a leader of LinkedIn's education team and a career coach to both military veterans and University of Michigan MBAs.

And I hate it. Because it doesn't have to be this way. Indeed, I've seen how a great coach can make all the difference to a struggling job seeker.

There's only one problem: Great coaching doesn't come cheap. Whether it's $500 to rewrite a resume or $100/hour for interview coaching, this pricing puts coaching out of reach for the very people it's intended to serve - *people looking for a job*.

Introducing the First Scalable Career Coach

At least this was the state of things in the fall of 2022.

That's when my boss, Sal Khan, told me about a conversation he had with the team at OpenAI.

"They're coming out with something huge," he said. "Something that will change education - and probably the world - forever."

Now, even working in Silicon Valley, I was skeptical. After all, I had just spent the last decade hearing about the magical Internet of Things, the wizardry of VR/AR, and the supposed power of cryptocurrency. And they had all failed to deliver on their hype, one after another. So it seemed unlikely that a small tech company like OpenAI would be able to really move the needle - let alone change the world.

And then I tried GPT–4.

Within minutes, it was clear that this new technology really would be able to change education (a personal tutor for every student!). And business (a personal copywriter for every professional!). And yes, maybe even the painful and lonely job searches we've all endured.

Because just by asking simple questions like "Give me feedback on my resume" or "Generate 5 interview questions for this job," I could produce better, more personalized feedback than any blog or online course could offer.

It was so eerily good, in fact, that it even rivaled the kind of bespoke advice I gave my individual clients. Which planted the seed of an idea:

What if I could combine everything I knew about the hidden world of Applicant Tracking Systems, LinkedIn algorithms, and interview evaluations with the power of this incredible new tool?

Introducing Career Coach GPT.

A complete, step-by-step process to get Jedi-level career coaching. But instead of paying thousands of dollars for it, you can leverage AI to get the coaching - and the job - you deserve for the price of this book.

Here's How It Works

To fully realize the power of Career Coach GPT, all you need to do is commit to taking action.

Because the beauty of being guided by an AI coach is you don't have to feel alone. You don't have to spend hours wading through blogs or getting stuck in your own head.

Instead, just follow each step and prompt in the forthcoming chapters and I guarantee you'll get farther, faster than you would have on your own.

And the first step is to choose your preferred tool. While I personally love ChatGPT Plus because it gives you access to the most powerful AI without any downtime, I recognize that shelling out money can be a challenge when you're looking for a new job.

So if you prefer, you're welcome to use any of the following free alternatives:

- Bing Chat
- Google Bard
- You.com

I've tried the prompts in this book with all of those models with similar levels of success. And I'm sure you'll discover even more after publication, given the incredible rate of change in this new space.

But whichever AI bot you prefer, please go ahead and fire it up now so you can start taking action immediately - and start getting results ASAP.

1) Find Your Path

As tempting as it is to dive right into building resumes and applying online, resist the temptation!

That's because here's the secret of all great job searches - whether they're AI-powered or not: **They're incredibly focused.**

While having a clear sense of where you're headed makes you more likely to actually get there, it's equally important for your audience: *Recruiters.*

After all, if you're a recruiter who's been tasked with finding a great Product Manager for your company, would you prefer someone whose application is all over the place? Or someone who's laser-focused?

Which means that if you want to win over this audience - and you definitely do - then you have to start with focus.

How Do I Follow My Passion?

Whether you're pursuing your 1st job or your 21st, it's easy to get tripped up at this stage.

There's so much conflicting advice out there:

- "Follow your passion!"
- "Follow the trends!"
- "Follow the money!!!"

And again, if you're searching on your own like most job-seekers, you can wind up getting stuck so deeply in your head that you never even get around to applying in the real world.

So to break through that deadlock, let's turn to AI for some concrete ideas and next steps.

[ ] Specifically, plug the following into your preferred chatbot:

> *Generate 10 specific job titles that could be a good fit for me based on:*
>
> *My Favorite Skills:*
>
> *My Interests:*
>
> *My Major:*
>
> *My Resume:*

Get Your Workbook!
Don't want to type these prompts into your favorite chatbot?

Me neither... 🙂

[ ] Just head over to <u>bit.ly/gptworkbook</u> (all lower-case) to grab your very own Career Coach GPT Workbook - including copies of all these prompts, instructions on how to get started, and more!

Note that you should only include the information that you want the AI to consider. So, for instance, a student who really wants to leverage their Sociology major but definitely doesn't want to go back to lifeguarding (their most recent job) should include their major but not their resume:

> *Generate 10 specific job titles that could be a good fit for me based on:*
>
> *My Favorite Skills: Research, Writing, Interview*

My Interests: Animals, Environment

My Major: Sociology

This produces a great list of roles that draw upon what gives the student energy - but doesn't typecast them as a student worker forever!

Generate 10 specific job titles that could be a good fit for me based on:
My Favorite Skills: Research, Writing, Interview
My Interests: Animals, Environment
My Major: Sociology

Based on your favorite skills, interests, and major, here are ten specific job titles that could be a good fit for you:

1. Environmental Researcher - Conduct research on environmental issues and write reports on findings.
2. Animal Welfare Advocate - Research animal welfare issues and advocate for policies and practices that improve animal welfare.
3. Environmental Journalist - Write articles and reports on environmental issues for newspapers, magazines, and websites.
4. Wildlife Biologist - Conduct research on animal behavior and habitat, and write reports on findings.
5. Environmental Policy Analyst - Research environmental policies and make recommendations for policy changes.
6. Animal Rights Campaigner - Advocate for animal rights through research and public awareness campaigns.
7. Environmental Educator - Develop and teach environmental education programs to raise awareness and promote sustainability.
8. Animal Behaviorist - Conduct research on animal behavior and write reports on findings.
9. Environmental Sociologist - Conduct research on environmental issues and analyze how social factors affect environmental problems.
10. Wildlife Conservationist - Conduct research on wildlife populations and develop strategies for their conservation.

On the other hand, an experienced professional may want to double-down on their existing career by including their Sales resume but not lead the AI astray by mentioning their long irrelevant Philosophy major:

Generate 10 specific job titles that could be a good fit for me based on:

My Favorite Skills: Sales, Presentations, Negotiations

My Interests: Education, Healthcare

My Resume: XXX

Now they get a hyper sales-relevant list that builds upon their existing experience without taking a detour to long-defunct parts of their CV:

1. Sales Manager for Healthcare Education Products
2. Director of Business Development for an Edtech Startup
3. Healthcare Sales Representative for Medical Devices
4. Presenter and Trainer for Healthcare Professionals
5. Negotiation Specialist for Pharmaceutical Sales
6. Business Development Manager for Healthcare Consulting Firm
7. Education Program Manager for Healthcare Providers
8. Sales Executive for Healthcare Information Technology
9. Education Consultant for Edtech Companies
10. Healthcare Business Development Director for a Marketing Agency.

Either way, the goal is to immediately break through the analysis paralysis and start thinking about concrete job titles. Especially since, as mentioned, that's the exact way recruiters see the world. So there's no point in focusing on abstract job categories ("I want to work in tech!") when you can immediately hone in on the language of your target audience.

How Can I Possibly Choose?

The next step where solo job-seekers tend to get stuck is the FOMO Phase. Once you've developed a list of potential jobs, it can be excruciating to choose a specific path - after all, they all seem so tempting.

But again, your trusty AI sidekick is here to help you break through.

Start by feeding it all the job titles that seem intriguing to you and ask the following:

> *Please tell me about a typical day for each of these job titles and the kinds of people who tend to enjoy them: INSERT TITLES*

 Please tell me about a typical day for each of these job titles and the kinds of people who tend to enjoy them: Environmental Researcher, Animal Welfare Advocate, Wildlife Biologist.

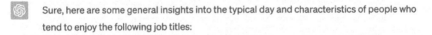 Sure, here are some general insights into the typical day and characteristics of people who tend to enjoy the following job titles:

Environmental Researcher:
A typical day for an Environmental Researcher may involve conducting fieldwork to collect environmental data, analyzing data in a laboratory setting, and writing reports or articles about their findings. They may also collaborate with other scientists, policymakers, and stakeholders to develop solutions to environmental issues. Environmental Researchers tend to enjoy working independently or in small teams, have a strong interest in science and the environment, and are detail-oriented and analytical. They may have a background in biology, chemistry, geology, or environmental science, and may work for government agencies, non-profit organizations, or consulting firms.

This test tackles the first underlying element of FOMO: *Ignorance.* Specifically, the lack of insider knowledge that makes every job look glamorous from the outside.

Because once you know what a job is really like, it can be easier to rule out if the work doesn't sound appealing or if it's not a good fit for your personality.

And then, to help break ties for any jobs that still seem like a good fit, try the following prompt:

Rank these jobs - INSERT TITLES - based on my:

Career Goals: INSERT GOALS

Qualifications: INSERT SKILLS + CREDENTIALS

 Rank these jobs - Environmental Researcher, Animal Welfare Advocate, Wildlife Biologist - based on my:
Career Goals: Maximize compensation
Qualifications: Sociology major with strong research, writing, and interview skills

 Based on your career goals and qualifications, the job titles can be ranked as follows, from highest to lowest:

1. Environmental Researcher - Environmental researchers are involved in a range of activities such as collecting and analyzing data, conducting research and developing reports on environmental issues. Your strong research and writing skills make you a good fit for this role. While compensation can vary depending on the organization you work for, it is typically higher than for roles in advocacy or conservation.
2. Wildlife Biologist - Wildlife biologists study the behavior, life cycles, and habitats of animals. Your skills in research and writing would be valuable for this position. While the compensation for this role may not be as high as for some other positions, it can still be competitive.
3. Animal Welfare Advocate - Animal welfare advocates work on promoting animal rights, conducting outreach, and building relationships with other organizations. Your strong writing and interview skills make you a good fit for this role. While the compensation for this role may be lower than for other positions, it can still be fulfilling if you have a passion for animal welfare.

Moving one step beyond personal preference, we now get down to the crucial questions of whether the job is right for your goals and whether you're actually right for the job.

So, for example, a new grad who has to pay off massive student loans and only has a BA may prove to be a poor fit for a professorship. But they could be an excellent fit for a well-paid Social Media Manager role that leverages their expertise in this space.

Alternatively, an experienced marketer who's looking for work-life balance may not connect with a COO role at a big company but could be a great CMO at a small nonprofit.

By now, you should have narrowed down your list of potential titles to a relatively small list. To get all the way to a singular focus, there's two strategies left - one online and one off.

The first technique involves returning to AI to get some homework. It turns out that ChatGPT and its brethren are great at making assignments - if you let them.

So feed your AI bot a prompt like the following:

What are three specific ways I can test my fit with each of the following roles: INSERT ROLES

What are three specific ways I can test my fit with each of the following roles: Environmental Researcher and Wildlife Biologist

 Here are three ways you can test your fit with the roles of Environmental Researcher and Wildlife Biologist:

For Environmental Researcher:

1. Volunteer with an environmental organization: One way to test your fit with the role of Environmental Researcher is to volunteer with an environmental organization. This will give you an opportunity to see firsthand what the work involves and whether it aligns with your interests and skills. You may be able to assist with research projects or data collection, which can give you an idea of what it's like to work in this field.
2. Attend industry events and conferences: Attending industry events and conferences can help you gain a better understanding of the field and the types of work that are involved. You may be able to attend talks or workshops on environmental research and speak with professionals in the field. This can help you determine whether this is a good fit for you.
3. Take relevant courses or workshops: Taking courses or workshops in environmental science or research can also help you test your fit with the role of Environmental Researcher. This can help you gain knowledge in the field and develop skills that are relevant to the work. Additionally, it can give you an idea of whether you enjoy the subject matter and would be interested in pursuing it further.

This will often give you homework that's highly actionable - whether it's reading specific resources or trying out specific experiences.

Alternatively, you can take on two birds with a single stone by turning to LinkedIn. That's because one of the most powerful techniques for applying to jobs is to get someone on the inside to refer you.

And so if you want to both learn about roles today and get ready to earn referrals tomorrow, reaching out to alumni from your alma mater can be a great place to start.

Here's how it works:

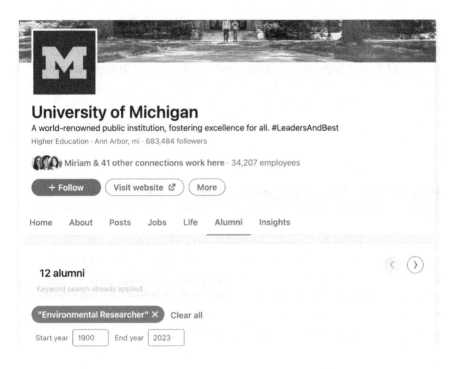

University of Michigan
A world-renowned public institution, fostering excellence for all. #LeadersAndBest
Higher Education · Ann Arbor, mi · 683,484 followers

Miriam & 41 other connections work here · 34,207 employees

+ Follow   Visit website ☑   More

Home   About   Posts   Jobs   Life   Alumni   Insights

12 alumni   ‹ ›
Keyword search already applied

"Environmental Researcher" ✕   Clear all

Start year | 1900 | End year | 2023 |

1. Start by searching for your university on LinkedIn

2. Click the Alumni tab on the university's page (this is the Alumni Tool I used to work on there!)

3. Now filter for alumni who work in your field of interest - and maybe companies and locations that interest you, too

4. Send a personalized connection request to the resulting alumni along the following lines:

    Hi NAME,

    I'm a fellow Wolverine/Spartan/etc. and I'm at a career crossroads. Specifically, I'm trying to decide whether to pursue your path. Would you be open to a 10-minute Zoom chat so I could learn from your journey?

Then, once you have a chat, you can ask them some of the questions we've already asked the AI ("What's a typical day like for you? What kind of person tends to be really happy in this role? Does it give you a chance to leverage X skills or achieve Y goals?"). But this time, instead of just getting a generic AI answer, you can get specific insider info to better shape your decision.

But What If I Just Can't Choose???

Ideally, you now have just a single job title to focus on. This not only will come in handy with your LinkedIn profile (since you only have one version to customize), but will also make your job search much easier because you won't have to constantly switch back-and-forth between different stories and skills as you make resumes and prepare for interviews.

That said, it's totally understandable if you just can't choose between a handful of fascinating opportunities. In that case, just remember your poor recruiter on the other side of the screen.

They're looking through thousands of resumes to find the handful of candidates who actually match the specific role they're looking to fill. And so getting generic, one-size-fits-all resumes actually makes their lives easier - by making it easier to reject you!

So to avoid that fate, be sure to generate customized resumes, cover letters, and interview stories for each role in the next few chapters.

While it might seem like a pain in the butt to do so, in the age of AI-powered job searching, it's actually more painful to settle for mediocre outcomes when you could have generated tailored applications in mere minutes.

Read on to learn how!

2) Shore Up Your LinkedIn Defenses

Before you go on offense with your AI-powered job applications, it makes sense to invest in playing defense on LinkedIn.

That's because at the same time that you're searching for jobs, recruiters are hungrily searching for you.

But they can't find you unless you have a LinkedIn profile that matches their searches.

So to ensure that your profile is working for you 24/7, let's invest a few minutes in making it shine right now.

Two Big Questions

Before we start digging into the LinkedIn algorithm, it's important to ask yourself two questions:

1. What is the specific title you want to be found for?

Of course, the answer is obvious if you narrowed down your focus to a single title in the last chapter.

But if you still have a couple roles you'd like to pursue, there are a few options to consider:

First, you could decide that one of the roles is way more appealing than the others and double-down on that on LinkedIn, even if you end up applying to a variety of roles behind-the-scenes.

Second, you could choose to pursue the roles serially instead of in parallel. For instance, you could go after the most interesting role (e.g., Product Manager) for 30 days and then switch to your back-up role (e.g., Product Marketing Manager) if you don't get many bites from recruiters.

Or third, you could list a variety of interests on LinkedIn that all cluster together. For example, if you're interested in both Account Executive and Business Development roles, it wouldn't raise too many red flags to list both of them. After all, they draw upon similar skillsets and so a professional who's qualified for one would likely be qualified for the other.

No matter which road you choose, just be sure to keep that focus in mind as we go through the rest of this chapter.

2. Are you free to broadcast that interest?

If you're currently a free agent, there's no reason you shouldn't share your interests on LinkedIn - and every reason you should!

After all, recruiters are on the prowl for your talent and every time they find you, that's one step closer to being off the market.

But what if you're currently employed? Is there some way to get the benefit of LinkedIn without being discovered by your boss?

It turns out there's two scenarios here:

On the one hand, if you're pursuing a role that's similar to your current one (e.g., you're a Developer but you want to become a Senior Developer), you can likely upgrade your profile without anyone noticing. That's because you're just elaborating on what everyone already knows about you.

On the other hand, if you're looking to drastically pivot your career (e.g., going from a Developer to an Accountant), you'll likely want to only apply two of the strategies described below -

Open to Work and Skills - since they won't be highly visible to your current employer.

How to Get Found

OK, with those constraints in mind, let's get down to the fun stuff: *Getting found by recruiters without lifting a finger.*

The trick here is just to reverse engineer all the things recruiters search for using LinkedIn Recruiter, their $10,000/seat/year tool that gives them access to all the talent on the platform.

As you'll notice, there are really only three things they search for that you can control: Job Title, Location, and Skills.

Let's tackle each of those in turn.

Job Title

Job title is easily the most important keyword a recruiter searches for. After all, remember their plight: Trying to find candidates who actually fit a role from thousands of resumes or millions of LinkedIn profiles.

So given that overwhelming haystack, why would they ever pursue a needle that doesn't at least match the most basic element - the job's title?

Now, if you're pivoting to a new job title, don't despair. There's an easy way around this Catch-22.

And it comes from the fact that if the Job Title is the recruiter's most important keyword, then your Headline is your most important profile section.

That's right - that tiny little blurb below your name has the most weight in the LinkedIn search algorithm. Because those sneaky LinkedIn engineers realized that its very brevity (limited to just 220 characters - shorter even than a Tweet!) makes it the hardest part of your profile to game. And so they've assigned it extra importance whenever a recruiter searches on the platform.

Marketing Director at Khan Academy | Passionate about AI EdTech + Career Development | Author of #1 LinkedIn Best-Seller on Amazon

Which means you absolutely need to nail your Headline. And AI is here to help you do just that with the following prompt:

> *Generate a 220 character LinkedIn profile Headline based on the following template, desired job title, and resume:*
>
> *Here's a headline template: DESIRED JOB (List "Seeking" if the candidate lacks experience) | RELEVANT SKILLS FOR JOB*
>
> *Here's the desired job title: INSERT JOB*
>
> *And here's the resume: INSERT RESUME*

 Generate a 220 character LinkedIn profile Headline based on the following template, desired job title, and resume:

Here's a headline template: DESIRED JOB (List "Seeking" if the candidate lacks experience) | RELEVANT SKILLS FOR JOB

Here's the desired job title: Product manager

And here's the resume:

 Product Manager | User Growth, Viral Marketing, Email Campaigns, Lead Generation, Retargeting, Product Development, SQL, Google Analytics

Now, even if you've never done the specific job before, you still show up on the recruiter's search because you've got their most important keyword right in your most important section. And the best part is that the LinkedIn algorithm doesn't distinguish between people who are currently doing the job vs. just seeking it!

Location

So let's say a recruiter has narrowed their search down to 100K candidates who are interested in a specific role. Next up, they want to focus their search on candidates who are local, since it's a lot easier to bring someone in from across town than across the world.

Even in this age of remote work, many recruiters will prefer to start with candidates in their area since it both reduces ongoing travel costs and increases flexibility if their employer ever decides to bring people back to the office full-time.

Which means that if you're already where you want to be - and your LinkedIn profile says that - you're golden.

But what about if you're sitting in San Antonio and want to land a job in San Francisco? Or you're on Oahu but need to move to Ohio?

In that case, don't assume that recruiters are psychic (they're not!) - and instead, help them understand your intentions.

Specifically, update your LinkedIn Location to where you want to be found - not where you're sitting right now.

City*

San Francisco Bay Area

That way, when recruiters search for talent in San Francisco or Ohio, your name rises to the top of their list. And if they reach out to you about an interview, you can let them know that you're planning to move just as soon as you land a job.

Which is a way more useful conversation than just sitting at home and moping to yourself about how recruiters never reach out to you from your desired location... :)

Skills

Now, our recruiter may be down to a more manageable list of 5K interested candidates in their desired location. But that's still too many to sort through - so they apply one last filter: Who can actually walk the talk, not just talk it?

Or more precisely, they search for Skills.

After all, anyone can claim to be a great Data Scientist. But if you don't have R, SQL, Python, and Tableau on your LinkedIn profile, chances are you're not quite ready for primetime.

So to demonstrate your worthiness, just focus on two questions:

1. What are the most important skills for my desired role?

2. Where can I list them on my profile?

To answer that first question, let's just put AI to work given that pattern-matching is one of its great strengths.

Here's a prompt to get started:

> *What are the 20 most common skills listed on job descriptions for JOB TITLE?*

What are the 20 most common skills listed on job descriptions for Product Manager?

 Here are the 20 most common skills listed on job descriptions for Product Manager, based on a review of several job postings:

1. Product development
2. Product management
3. Agile methodology
4. Project management
5. Business analysis
6. Market research
7. Data analysis
8. Strategic planning
9. Cross-functional collaboration
10. Roadmap creation
11. Product launch
12. Competitive analysis
13. User experience (UX)
14. Design thinking
15. Customer needs assessment
16. Pricing strategy
17. Product positioning
18. Market segmentation
19. Sales enablement
20. Communication skills

And just like that, you now have a list of the skills you should get credit for - assuming you have them.

Which leads us to our second question: "Where should you put them?"

By far, the easiest section of your profile to update is your Skills section. That's because you can flat-out list up to 50 skills without any fancy writing.

So immediately go to that section and list out as many of the AI-generated skills as you can rightfully claim.

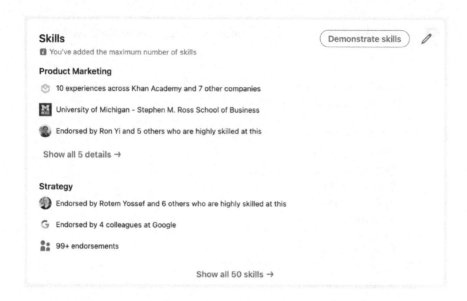

Skills

ℹ️ You've added the maximum number of skills

Product Marketing

🔶 10 experiences across Khan Academy and 7 other companies

Ⓜ️ University of Michigan - Stephen M. Ross School of Business

👤 Endorsed by Ron Yi and 5 others who are highly skilled at this

Show all 5 details →

Strategy

👤 Endorsed by Rotem Yossef and 6 others who are highly skilled at this

Ⓖ Endorsed by 4 colleagues at Google

👥 99+ endorsements

Show all 50 skills →

Demonstrate skills ✏️

But note that the LinkedIn algorithm isn't only interested in matching the desired skills - it also wants skill density.

In other words, it feels more confident recommending your profile to a recruiter if you have multiple instances of a given skill.

So the next obvious location for these critical keywords is your Experience section. After all, that's where you honed these skills, so you might as well incorporate them.

To do so, you could either painstakingly try to find skills to add to each of your resume bullet points - or let AI get it done for you in minutes.

All you need to do is run this prompt:

Please incorporate the following keywords into my existing resume bullet points.

Keywords:

Bullet Points:

Please incorporate the following keywords into my existing resume bullet points.
Keywords: Product development, Agile methodology
Bullet Points: ● Launched the world's first site to help non-coders land tech jobs; clients have earned offers ranging from Google to Spotify
● Built a subscriber list of 10K+ in a brand-new vertical, all with no marketing budget
● Earned features in Forbes, Fast Company, Lifehacker, Business Insider, and USA Today 2014-2015

Fidelis - VP, Marketing
● Utilized agile methodology to build a lead generation team and process from scratch, growing sales pipeline from 30 to 300 opportunities in two months ($40M in weighted value)
● Developed and executed product development strategy based on cross-platform ad testing, which included launching a retargeting campaign across email, web, and social, generating 3x industry-standard CTRs and leading to final round presentations
● Secured features in Forbes, Fast Company, Lifehacker, Business Insider, and USA Today through effective product development and marketing tactics.

The only catch is that AI has a tendency to "hallucinate" (yes, that's the technical term!) when pushed to generate new copy (vs. just stating well-trod facts). So please be sure to review the output carefully for accuracy before pasting to LinkedIn.

And then finally, there's one big remaining section that's unique to LinkedIn: Your About section.

While this section may be a bit mysterious ("About... What?"), see it for what it really is: 2,000 completely open characters you can do whatever you want with!

And, as with everything on LinkedIn, don't be fooled into thinking that these are optional characters to use or not.

Instead, keep your eyes on the prize and leverage them to get found using this prompt:

> *Generate a 2,000 character LinkedIn profile About section based on the following template, desired job title, and resume.*
>
> *Here's a template:*
>
> *Start with an opening sentence that states the candidate's focus on their desired job title.*
>
> ▶ *Pull out a relevant bullet from their resume*
>
> ▶ *Pull out a second relevant bullet from their resume*
>
> ▶ *Pull out a third relevant bullet from their resume*
>
> *Specialties: List the most relevant skills for the desired job from their resume*
>
> *Here's the desired job title:*
>
> *And here's the resume:*

Product Manager with a proven ability to drive massive user growth and deliver bottom line impact across B2C and B2B tech. Highlights include:

▶ Built teams that drove 100%+ Y/Y user growth at both tech giants and VC-funded startups
▶ Launched world-class campaigns with coverage in The New York Times and LinkedIn's most-watched video of all time
▶ Delivered substantial bottom line impact, from building a $40M lead pipeline to helping an edtech startup close its first $1M in sales

Specialties: Product development, Agile methodology, Email Marketing, Content Marketing, PPC, Social Media, SEO, Lead Generation, SQL, HTML/CSS, Google Analytics, AdWords, Retargeting, Salesforce

But What If I Don't Have All/Any of These Skills?

All of the above assumes that you're actually a decent fit for the role based on your research in Chapter 1.

But what if you don't match all of the skills? Are you out of the running???

First, recognize that recruiters actually don't want you to be 100% qualified.

Check out this fascinating research from TalentWorks that suggests 50% qualified candidates have the best chance of getting interviews - and that your chances actually decrease beyond that.

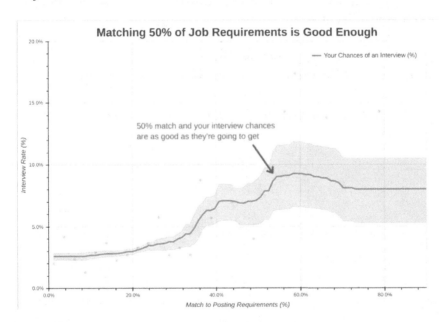

What gives???

It turns out that recruiters are, again, behaving incredibly rationally. Because they don't have time to waste on candidates who aren't serious about a role, a 100% qualified candidate is actually a liability. What if they go through the entire interview process, chewing up limited time and interview slots, only to bail for a more challenging job at the very last second? What a waste!

Whereas a 50% qualified candidate is the perfect balance between being able to come in and hit the ground running - but still hungry enough to keep pushing well beyond their start. In other words, the exact kind of candidate who's likely to get and accept a job offer!

So bottom-line: If you can match roughly 50% of the desired skills, you should absolutely go for it!

But what if your match rate is way lower? Or... gulp... you don't match any skills at all???

In that case, you definitely have more work to do. But again, AI is standing by to support your success with this prompt:

> *What are the specific fastest and cheapest ways to learn SKILL?*

What are the specific fastest and cheapest ways to learn Agile?

 Here are some specific ways to learn Agile quickly and inexpensively:

1. Online Courses: There are a plethora of free and low-cost online courses that teach Agile methodologies. Some popular platforms include Coursera, Udemy, edX, and LinkedIn Learning.
2. Books: There are many books that offer an introduction to Agile, including "Agile Estimating and Planning" by Mike Cohn, "User Story Mapping" by Jeff Patton, and "Scrum: The Art of Doing Twice the Work in Half the Time" by Jeff Sutherland.
3. Attend Workshops and Meetups: Joining local Agile communities and attending meetups and workshops can be a great way to learn Agile. These events are often free or low-cost and can provide opportunities to network with other professionals in the field.
4. Online Resources: There are numerous blogs, podcasts, and YouTube channels that offer insights into Agile. Some popular resources include Agile Alliance, Agile Manifesto, Agile Coach's Corner Podcast, and Scrum.org.
5. Practice: One of the best ways to learn Agile is through practice. Start by implementing Agile methodologies in your own work, even if it's just for small projects. Experiment with different Agile frameworks such as Scrum, Kanban, or Lean, and learn from your successes and failures.

Instead of wasting your time and money by sending you back for a master's degree, you'll often get recommendations of online courses or projects that can upskill you in weeks, not years.

ChatGPT FTW!

How to Get Chosen

So you've conquered the first big LinkedIn obstacle: *Getting found by recruiters.*

Which means there's only one last hurdle to overcome: *Getting chosen.*

Because as all-powerful as recruiters might seem, even they have their LinkedIn kryptonite: **InMails.**

Specifically, because LinkedIn wants to both increase the perceived value of these private messages and limit the amount of spam sent out, they limit recruiters to about 30 InMails/month on average. Yes, even the recruiters paying $10K/year. See, it's good to be a monopoly... :)

That said, this isn't just a problem for recruiters, it's also a problem for you. Because it means that even when recruiters find your profile, they have to be very picky about whether to use one of their scarce InMails on you.

Luckily, there's one extra factor that helps both parties. Because LinkedIn wants to incentivize recruiters to reach out to serious candidates (a win-win for both sides), it makes recruiters a deal: "If you reach out to a candidate who's serious enough to respond to your InMail, we'll refund that credit." And so, a savvy recruiter who only goes after the most serious candidates can stretch their InMail budget from 30/month to 300 or more!

To see how they do this, check out the three bonus filters they can apply in LinkedIn Recruiter:

1. Open to Work

OK, back to our poor recruiter friend. They're down to 1,000 local candidates who all have the right skills but that's still way too many for their limited InMail budget.

So why waste a single InMail on someone who's not seriously looking?

To distinguish between serious and uninterested candidates, they'll first filter for Open to Work. This is the signal you can activate on your profile specifying the kinds of roles and locations that interest you.

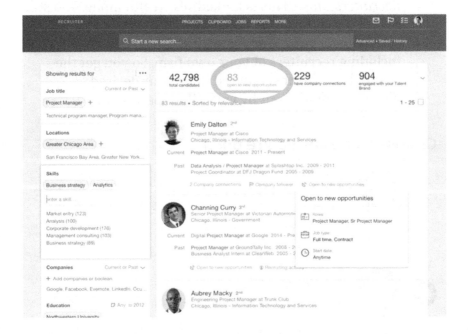

So because it's such an easy cut for recruiters to make, it's critical to turn this on as soon as you can. Because even if you're currently employed, it comes in two flavors:

- *#OpenToWork* - This puts a green banner on your profile photo that lets everyone in your network know that you're actively looking. And while it might feel a little scary to put that out there so vividly, LinkedIn's own research shows that candidates with this signal are more likely to discover new opportunities - likely because of the power of weak ties (i.e., the sociological phenomenon whereby people at the periphery of your network are more likely to introduce you to new opportunities than friends and family - something LinkedIn and MIT validated with a 20M-user study recently[1]).

- *Recruiters Only* - This is LinkedIn's stealth mode. You still get to send this powerful signal to recruiters at other companies - but it can't be seen by anyone else, including recruiters at your own firm. So you get the best of both worlds: Filtered in by your desired audience, filtered out by your HR department!

Choose who sees you're open

All LinkedIn members
This also includes recruiters and people at your current company.

Adds the #OpenToWork photo frame.

Recruiters only
People using LinkedIn Recruiter.

We take steps to not show recruiters at your current company, though can't guarantee complete privacy.

So bottom-line: Even if you had to skip much of the above advice due to your current employment, Open to Work is the one step that every job-seeker should leverage!

2. In Your Network

Now our recruiter is down to 500 candidates, so they keep on pushing. And, specifically, they realize the following: "My InMails are more likely to get a response if the candidate knows someone at my company. After all, they'll have more context about the firm - plus, I'll have someone I can reach out to for an intro."

---

1 https://news.mit.edu/2022/weak-ties-linkedin-employment-0915

So they apply this filter to only show candidates with a connection at their firms:

Now, I know what you're thinking: "Ugh, Jeremy - everything was going so smoothly. Now I have to stop everything to go have coffee with people at all the companies I like?"

No way.

If you've learned anything about me so far, I'm all about efficiency. And let's be honest, I'm pretty darn lazy, too... :)

So to my way of thinking, why waste weeks and months building new relationships when you can get credit for the ones you already have?

Here's what I mean:

- The average human knows about 5,000 people over the course of a lifetime.

- Yet, the average LinkedIn member only has about 50 connections.

- Which means he/she doesn't get credit for thousands of actual IRL connections every time a recruiter applies that filter.

So, to close this gap as fast as possible, here's a little shortcut:

1. Just select My Network in LinkedIn's top menu

2. Look for the "Add personal contacts" section on the left-hand side.

Add personal contacts

We'll periodically import and store your contacts
to help you and others connect. You choose who
to connect to and who to invite. **Learn more**

> Your email address

(Continue)

More options

3. Import your address books - including both any email contacts (Gmail, Yahoo!, etc.) and your phone's address book (using the LinkedIn app)

4. Connect with everyone that you already know - even if it was just a brief correspondence (check out that weak ties research if you want to see how powerful these connections can be!)

Bam! Just like that, you'll be able to grow your network by 2X or more. Which means that every time recruiters at your dream companies filter for people connected to their firms, you have a way better shot of knowing someone on the inside!

3. Engaged with Your Talent Brand

At long last, the recruiter is down to about 100 candidates and closing in on just the 5–10 worthy of those precious InMails (remember that recruiters are always juggling multiple roles so can't afford to blow their whole budget on a single search).

To get all the way to the promised land, they just need one last signal of interest - and one last filter.

And sure enough, LinkedIn has a super simple one: *Who actually likes my company?*

Even though it appears under the totally abstract title of "Engaged with Your Talent Brand," this basically means "Hey, LinkedIn - just show me the people following my company."

Which means your last job is probably the simplest: Literally just click "Follow" on the Company Page of every firm you're interested in.

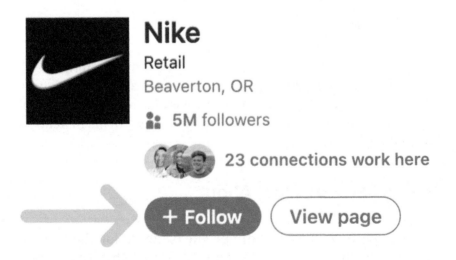

And as tedious as that sounds, AI is here to help with the following prompt:

Generate a list of the 100 top employers of X job title in Y industry and Z location.

 Generate a list of the 100 top employers of Product Managers in EdTech in Silicon Valley.

 As an AI language model, I don't have real-time data or access to specific lists of employers. However, I can provide you with a general list of well-known companies in Silicon Valley that are involved in the EdTech sector. Keep in mind that the rankings and positions of these companies may vary over time. Here's a list of 100 companies that are prominent in the EdTech industry and might employ product managers in Silicon Valley:

1. Coursera
2. Khan Academy
3. Udemy
4. Edmodo
5. Chegg
6. LinkedIn Learning
7. Udacity
8. Lynda.com
9. Quizlet
10. Thinkific
11. Pluralsight
12. Duolingo

Of course, you can leave off industry or location if you're agnostic to those things. But whatever your parameters, you can now fly through this list and rest easy knowing that for the rest of your career, you'll be filtered in by these firms instead of filtered out!

Wait a Second! What About...

As far as putting your LinkedIn profile on autopilot, the above tasks are really the most critical ones. After all, they're the steps that are baked into the very Recruiter tool that decides your fate.

However, let me be honest with you: Even before I was a ChatGPT fanboy, I was a hardcore LinkedIn fanboy. Not only did I turn down job offers from Amazon and Microsoft to work there, but I co-wrote the best-selling book on the topic and am now the official LinkedIn trainer everywhere from Harvard Business School to the Canadian Olympic Committee.

So let me just geek out for a sec with three optional but powerful bonus hacks:

1. Pictures > Words.

As powerful as keywords are for getting found by LinkedIn's algorithm, humans are still in charge of making the final decision about who gets interviewed (at least until GPT–13 comes out... ;). And what do we know about humans? We're an incredibly visual species - as evidenced by the fact that we drew stories on cave walls long before we invented language.

In other words: *Don't ignore the power of visuals to sway your ultimate decision-makers.*

This plays out in two particular sections:

A) Profile Photos

Your LinkedIn profile "Holy Trinity" reflects the three things recruiters always see whenever your profile comes up:

- Your Headline
- Your Location
- Your Profile Photo

Jeremy Schifeling

Marketing Director at Khan Academy | Passionate about AI EdTech +
Career Development | Author of #1 LinkedIn Best-Seller on Amazon

Talks about #edtech, #linkedin, and #careeradvice

San Francisco Bay Area · **Contact info**

Having already covered the first two, let's focus on the third.
Especially since eye-tracking studies of recruiters suggest they
spend a disproportionate amount of time checking out your
photo.

And what are they looking for?

Likely, the same things we all look for in faces: *Is this person
friend or foe? Trustworthy or unreliable?*

Which means that your photo should be optimized to send
those exact signals by:

- **Closely cropping it around your head and shoulders.**
  Since humans prefer to gaze at faces over just about
  anything else, you don't want to waste your scarce pixels
  on your shoes, the background scenery, or someone
  else's shoulders!

- **Showing off a Duchenne smile.** This is the
  psychological term for a smile that requires your
  autonomic nervous system to start firing (upturned lips,
  dimpling in the cheeks, wrinkling around the eye) -

which, at least in Western culture, creates the perception of a genuine and trustworthy individual.[2] As compared to the forced "Botox smile" you see on so many profiles - smiling teeth contrasting with a staid face.

- **Dressing for the tribe you want to enter.** Since all of these judgments are happening in the blink of an eye, you want to immediately send the signal that you fit with the job and company you want to join. And one of the easiest signals of fit (or lack thereof!) is your attire. So check out some profiles of people with the role you want and get a sense of whether formal, corporate attire is essential (e.g., investment banking, management consulting) or frowned upon (e.g., software development, tech startups). And then dress the part!

Jeff Weiner · 2nd

Executive Chairman at LinkedIn / Founding Partner Next Play Ventures

Of course, this wouldn't be an AI book if we didn't include a little technological support for these human decisions. So if you're unsure how else to optimize your photo, head over to snappr.com/photo-analyzer. Snappr's AI will grab your photo straight from LinkedIn and then analyze every element based

---

[2] https://www.psychologicalscience.org/observer/the-psychological-study-of-smiling

on the latest research into how humans interpret faces. All for free! Isn't technology great? ;)

B) Cover Photos

As important as your profile photo is, your Cover Photo - that big rectangular box at the top of your profile - takes up even more precious digital real estate.

And so it would be a real shame to just leave a bland, gray box where you could be emphasizing your personal brand with a powerful visual.

To do this, just leverage AI to generate visual symbols of your positioning with a prompt like this:

Please generate 10 ideas for a photo of X role in action.

 Generate 10 ideas for photos of Product Managers in action

 Certainly! Here are 10 ideas for photos capturing Product Managers in action:

1. A Product Manager leading a brainstorming session with a whiteboard full of ideas and team members engaged in discussion.
2. A Product Manager conducting user research, interviewing a customer and taking notes.
3. A Product Manager collaborating with designers and engineers, reviewing wireframes or prototypes on a large screen.
4. A Product Manager presenting a product roadmap to a group of stakeholders, pointing to key milestones and features.

You'll get back a list of ideas (e.g., a whiteboard to represent a Product Manager's brainstorming work) that you can then plug straight into pexels.com - a royalty-free archive of beautiful photos that can make your profile sizzle right away!

Now, when a recruiter lands on your profile, instead of being greeted by a generic background, they'll know immediately that they've found a match for their specific search.

2. Actions > Words

As important as your own signals are to LinkedIn recruiters, the actions that you and others around you take can be even more important. Here are two examples:

A) Open to Work vs. InMail Responses

While "Open to Work" is a great initial signal of your interest in new roles, LinkedIn has trained its algorithm to prioritize your on-site actions over your mere claims.

Specifically, because recruiters have such a limited number of InMails to send, LinkedIn's algorithm bumps up users who respond to InMails frequently and quickly - and bumps down those who do the opposite. That way, any user that recruiters see at the top of their screens is likely to be an engaged reviewer of InMails - not just an InMail dilettante… ;)

So to make sure that this prioritization works in your favor, be sure to respond to every InMail you get right away. Even if it's a spam message, just click the "No thanks…" button. That way, the algorithm starts to tag you as someone who's actually engaged on the site - not just an "Open to Work" tease!

B) Endorsements vs. Recommendations

The same thing goes for Endorsements vs. Recommendations. While the former might seem enticing to collect because they're so quick and easy, their very lightness makes them useless to recruiters. After all, if 100 friends all endorsed you for "Leadership," does that actually make you a good leader? Or just popular???

Todd also knows about...

4 Molecular Gastronomy		55 Cloud Computing		11 Sauces				
6 Psychic Readings		12 Political Asylum		6 Wine Tasting				
70 Security		23 Yak Shaving		52 BGP		46 Start-ups		
63 Linux		34 Rhinoceros		30 Routing		36 Network Architecture		
25 Pork		17 Peering		24 Unix		20 Open Source		
18 System Architecture		15 Retaining Walls		16 Network Security				
34 TCP/IP		7 Network Design		8 IP		7 Network Engineering		
5 Internet Services		7 DNS		12 Strategy		5 Wikipedia		
8 Cultural Awareness		3 Reliability Engineering		11 Data Center				
8 Terracotta		7 Scalability		10 Sandwiches		3 Visio		

Whereas if your boss or client writes a glowing Recommendation about your leadership traits and cites real stories, even a single genuine Recommendation can count for a whole lot more than 100 insincere Endorsements.

Martina Valkovicova [in] · 1st
It is not what the world holds for you, it is what you bring to it.
April 9, 2023, Martina was Jeremy's client

How do I even start to describe Jeremy's contagious positive energy and vast knowledge? Over the years, Jeremy has provided an immense value to our students and also to our team. His sessions on LinkedIn are still evaluated as one of the best career workshops by our students. I love running ideas by him and ask for his advice - from new trends in career services to strategy. I leverage the book Linked in my relat ...see more

And the proof is in the pudding: Even though recruiters can't filter for Endorsements inside LinkedIn Recruiter (given the lack of credibility), Recommendations are shown at the very top of candidate profiles since they allow recruiters to quickly assess a user's legitimacy.

So the power of Recommendations should now be clear. But how do you actually get one?

Even if you and a former boss or client haven't been in-touch recently, AI is here to help you wordsmith your way to the perfect ask:

Generate a LinkedIn Recommendation request for my former boss/client, X. Please use a friendly but grateful and respectful tone. Keep the message under 500 characters.

 Generate a LinkedIn Recommendation request for my former boss, Sarah. Please use a friendly but grateful and respectful tone. Keep the message under 500 characters.

 Dear Sarah,

I hope this message finds you well. It's been a while since we last worked together, and I wanted to express my gratitude for the valuable experience and guidance you provided during our time at [company name]. Your leadership and support greatly contributed to my professional growth. If you would consider writing a LinkedIn recommendation for me, I would be truly honored. Thank you for everything!

Warm regards,
[Your Name]

3. Words > Words

Given that words drive LinkedIn SEO, it should come as no surprise that more words beat fewer. And while we've already covered how to leverage every last word in your Headline, About section, and just about everywhere else on your profile, there are two places off your profile where words also matter:

A) On Google

One of the very best things about LinkedIn is that you get two big SEO plays for the price of one. That's because updating your LinkedIn profile not only increases the odds you'll be found on the site - but also on the granddaddy of all sites: Google.

After all, if you search for just about any person in the world, their very first Google result will be their LinkedIn profile. Which means that for recruiters, hiring managers, and headhunters who are also prowling Google, you'll still be front-and-center.

The only catch is that you have to actually give Google access to your LinkedIn data - something that many users have turned off given understandable privacy fears about social networks.

But here's the good news: *LinkedIn isn't like other social networks.* Frankly, it's boring, well-lit, and generally not the kind of place where people go to ruin others' lives and careers... :)

So when you build your profile here, it's the good kind of information that you want to be everywhere - the kind of information *you* control and that's not posted *about* you.

Which means you should be sure to click "Edit public profile & URL" in the top right-hand corner of your profile and confirm that you've made your profile visible before moving on.

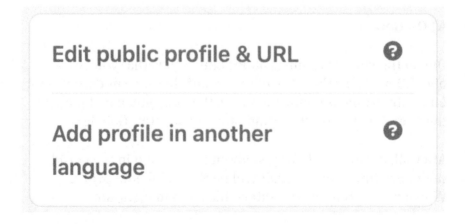

👁 Edit Visibility

You control your profile's appearance for people who are not signed in to LinkedIn. The limits you set here affect how your profile appears on search engines, profile badges, and permitted services like Outlook. Learn more

Your profile's public visibility	On ⬤

B) In Other Countries

The biggest constraint on words on LinkedIn isn't your actual profile. After all, you're no longer limited to a single 8.5 x 11" piece of paper.

Instead, it's the fact that you can only have one profile - vs. all the multiple copies of your resume that you're used to making for different roles.

And while we've already talked about how this can lead to compromises in your Headline, there is one group of LinkedIn users who are entitled to a bonus profile: *Multilingual job-seekers.*

Specifically, if you're searching for jobs in two or more parts of the world where different languages are spoken, you can go to "Add profile in another language" at the top of your profile and build a second version.

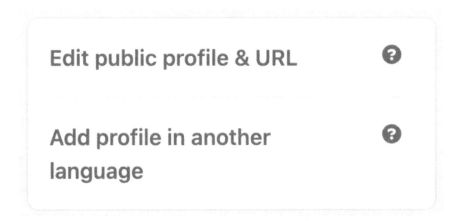

Edit public profile & URL

Add profile in another language

For instance, let's say you're looking for Finance jobs in NYC and Consulting jobs back home in São Paulo. In this case, your standard English-language profile can be optimized for Finance, while your new Portuguese profile can be optimized for Consulting.

Language of new profile*

Portuguese ▼

Start your Portuguese profile with your name and headline

First Name*   Last Name*

Jeremy   Schifeling

Headline*

Consultor

And the best part is that the recruiters in the two countries will have no idea that your other profile/interest exists, since they'll only be shown the version that matches their language.

Voila: Two profiles! And twice as many words!!! :)

3) Go on the Offense with Your Resume

With your LinkedIn profile defenses activated, it's time to go on offense. And that means loading up your biggest artillery: *Your resume!*

How Resumes Are Evaluated

Let's kick things off with the biggest mistake that job-seekers make: Not understanding what's happening on *the other side of the screen* when you apply online.

To remedy that issue, let me ask you some questions about the lucky recipient of your resume, the recruiter. And then stay tuned for pop quizzes throughout this chapter to keep you energized, given that it's the longest, toughest part of the book! ⚡

OK, here's goes:

If you had to guess how many resumes the average recruiter is juggling at once, where would you peg it? As low as 100? As high as 10,000? Somewhere in the middle?

HOW MANY RESUMES IS THE AVERAGE RECRUITER **JUGGLING** AT ANY TIME?

- A) 100

- B) 1,000

- C) 10,000

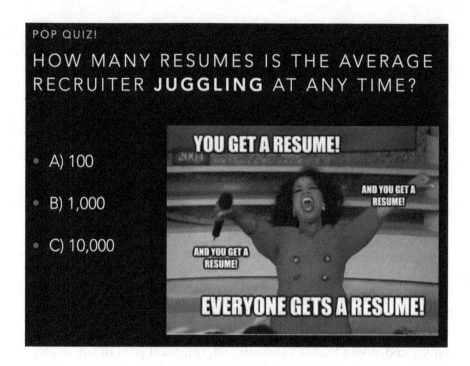

Well, as someone who used to recruit at Teach For America, I'm sad to say the answer is closer to 10K.

That's because the average recruiter is juggling about 40 open roles at any given time - and the average job posting attracts 250 resumes. So do the math and you're talking about a really tough job.

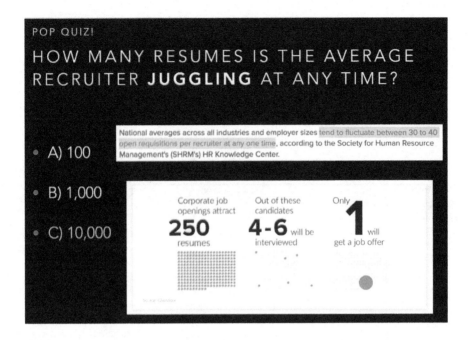

Which raises the next question: *How does a single recruiter actually read 10,000 resumes?*

Perhaps it's the miracle of caffeine or those little talent elves that come out after dark and sort through all the applications? Unfortunately, as you've probably guessed by now, the reality is that even the world's most efficient recruiter doesn't read every resume.

In fact, the world's most efficient recruiter likely reads very few actual resumes because of the modern miracle that is the Applicant Tracking System. Also called an ATS, an Applicant Tracking System is basically a special database for job applications. And even if you didn't realize it, every time you've applied for a job online, your resume has gone right into an ATS.

We'll go into greater detail on what happens next later but the key thing to understand is that the ATS automatically compares your application to the most important skills in the job description and decides if there's a strong match. If not, chances are no recruiter will ever read it - and you'll soon be getting one of those "There were so many qualified candidates..." emails.

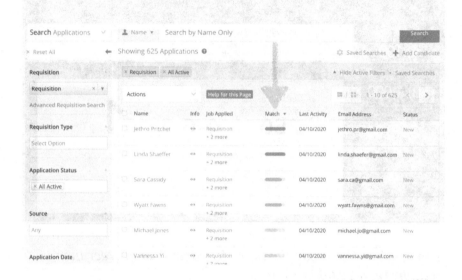

And even if you do pass the ATS test, what's your guess for how much time the recruiter will spend reading your resume?

6 seconds? 60 seconds? Somewhere in the middle?

HOW MANY **SECONDS** DO RECRUITERS SPEND REVIEWING A RESUME, ON AVERAGE?

- A) 6

- B) 25

- C) 60

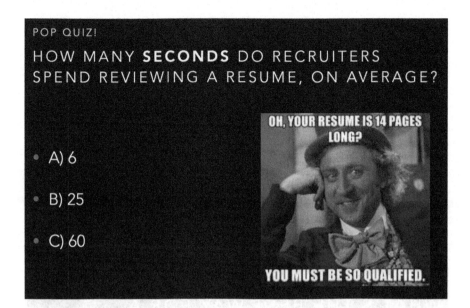

Well, hopefully you're getting the gist now. Recruiters have such a crushing workload that the average review is a mere blink of the eye.

HOW MANY **SECONDS** DO RECRUITERS SPEND REVIEWING A RESUME, ON AVERAGE?

- A) 6

- B) 25

- C) 60

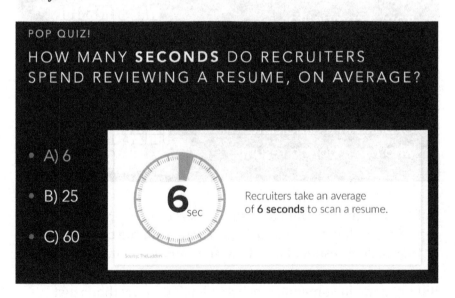

6 sec

Recruiters take an average of **6 seconds** to scan a resume.

Source: TheLadders

But don't freak out - I'm going to teach you exactly what they look for in those 6 seconds so you can maximize every precious tick. So stay tuned for that shortly.

But in the meantime, here's the most important question of all: Because recruiters are humans and not robots, they care about *not getting fired* just like you and me. So what do you think is the easiest way for a recruiter to get canned?

Do you think the surest path to disaster is bringing in a candidate from a competitor? Or offering an interview to someone with a boring resume?

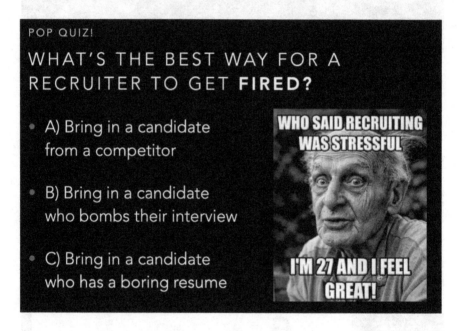

POP QUIZ!

WHAT'S THE BEST WAY FOR A RECRUITER TO GET **FIRED?**

- A) Bring in a candidate from a competitor

- B) Bring in a candidate who bombs their interview

- C) Bring in a candidate who has a boring resume

WHO SAID RECRUITING WAS STRESSFUL

I'M 27 AND I FEEL GREAT!

Nah - those things could actually get a recruiter promoted, especially if they poach a rockstar away from the competition or that boring resume has all the right things on it.

But bringing in someone who can't hack it - now that's just *unforgivable*.

WHAT'S THE BEST WAY FOR A RECRUITER TO GET **FIRED?**

- A) Bring in a candidate from a competitor

- B) Bring in a candidate who bombs their interview

I WILL GET MY CANDIDATE TO THE 6TH AND FINAL INTERVIEW

- C) Bring in a candidate who has a boring resume

Because not only does that waste the time of all the bigwigs in the interview room, it also raises this question: "You had 250 resumes - why didn't you pick the obvious candidates who could do this job in their sleep? *Why did you take a chance on this weirdo?*"

And with that recruiter nightmare firmly planted in your mind, let's wrap up this tour of their world with three key insights:

THE FOUNDATIONAL INSIGHTS

1. RECRUITERS' JOBS ARE **HARD.**

2. THEY USE TECHNOLOGY TO MAKE THEM **EASIER.**

3. THEY ARE MASSIVELY **RISK AVERSE.**

1. Recruiters' Jobs Are Hard

First of all, it should be painfully clear by now that recruiters have super tough jobs. So start with a little empathy for where they're coming from before you curse the recruiters of the world after your next rejection.

2. They Use Technology To Make Them Easier

Speaking of empathy, imagine what you would do if you were in their seats. Faced with 10,000 resumes, you'd turn to technology too - just like you're turning to technology by reading this book. So don't look at the ATS as a cop-out, so much as an acknowledgment that we live in a world where workers have to do more with less. And so once you understand how the game works, you can play by those rules with the best of them.

3. They Are Massively Risk Averse

And then finally, if you really do a Vulcan mind meld with the recruiter on the other side of the screen, you'll understand why it pays to be risk averse. Just like the old saying goes: No one ever got fired for buying IBM no matter how unsexy, and no recruiter ever got fired for bringing in candidates who were obviously qualified - even if they're a little boring.

So the last step is to go beyond just understanding these things and to put these insights to work for you in the form of the 3 Resume Commandments.

THE 3 RESUME COMMANDMENTS

1. MAKE THE RECRUITER'S JOB **EASY**.

2. DESIGN YOUR RESUME FOR **TECHNOLOGY**.

3. BECOME THE **OBVIOUS CHOICE**.

1. Make The Recruiter's Job Easy

If recruiters have a tough job, it's your job to make it easier. Especially because if you show them love, they'll tend to return it many times over. So as you spend time working on your application, never let that poor recruiter and their needs stray far from your thoughts.

2. Design Your Resume For Technology

And then, as you start to write, don't just choose your words arbitrarily. Think specifically of the ATS and its insatiable hunger for specific words straight from the job description. Because once you do that, the right words become incredibly obvious.

3. Become the Obvious Choice

And lastly, speaking of obvious, that's exactly what you need to project to recruiters. Even if you're starting your career or changing paths, think about what an easy IBM-like choice would look like in your desired space. And then move heaven and earth to make yourself that obvious, default choice. The one that won't just keep recruiters from getting fired - but might even earn them a promotion!

If you can bring those three commandments to everything you do in this chapter, you'll be golden. **So let's get started!**

Get Your Template

Because this book is all about action, let's get you started with a resume template.

Now, because you're clearly a discerning resume author, you may be leaning towards one of those newfangled templates with pie charts, rating systems, and the works. But based on what we just talked about in the last section, why do you think that might be a bad idea?

Does it have to do with the technology, the human recruiter, or just pure tradition?

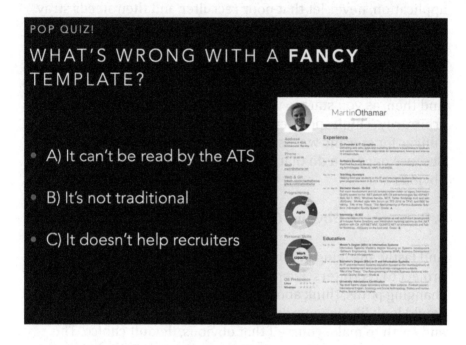

POP QUIZ!

WHAT'S WRONG WITH A **FANCY** TEMPLATE?

- A) It can't be read by the ATS

- B) It's not traditional

- C) It doesn't help recruiters

Well, as snazzy as a fancy template may look to a human recruiter, chances are they'll never get their hands on it because it will be screened out immediately by the ATS.

WHAT'S WRONG WITH A **FANCY** TEMPLATE?

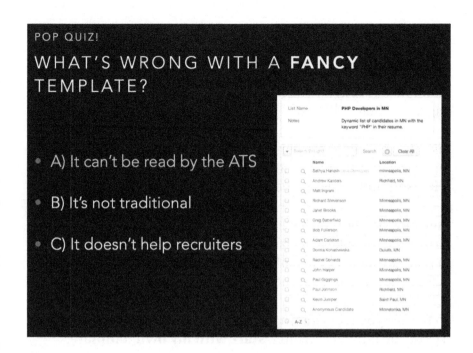

- A) It can't be read by the ATS

- B) It's not traditional

- C) It doesn't help recruiters

"Why," you ask? Do Applicant Tracking Systems have some kind of chip on their shoulder when it comes to pie charts?

Nope - it's simple Programming 101. Because the ATS has to be trained by its engineers where to scrape information from - things like your Name, Location, Experience, and Skills - these systems are trained almost exclusively on the standard resumes that make up 99% of applications.

While the engineers could have tried to train the systems on all the weirdo resume designs under the sun, all that extra effort would make almost no difference to compatibility. And to be honest, Applicant Tracking Systems aren't super high-tech to begin with - at least not like the AI you've got on your side!

So rather than pay hundreds of dollars for a gorgeous resume that never gets read, ditch the fancy format and go a little more traditional. But just to be clear: *That doesn't mean you should grab the first template you find in Microsoft Word.*

Why?

While playing it safe might ensure that your resume will be scanned correctly by the ATS, think about the problem with the engineers behind Word.

Just like the engineers behind Applicant Tracking Systems don't know the first thing about fancy resumes, the engineers at Microsoft don't have a clue how recruiters think.

And specifically, they have no clue that a recruiter who's struggling to make a decision in six seconds doesn't have time to read through a bunch of random education and coursework before they get to what the candidate can really do.

So to save you from getting automatically rejected by either the ATS or the human recruiter, **start with my own template.**

Not just because I've built it specifically for both the ATS and recruiter's needs, but because it gets results. Not only is this the exact resume that earned me offers at Google, Amazon, and Apple - but it's now been used over 500 times to land jobs across candidates and industries.

And why does it work so well? We'll, let's go back to those 3 resume commandments:

1. **If you want to make a recruiter's job easier,** don't make them guess whether you're a fit - spell it out right at the top. And don't make their tired eyes bleed by cramming everything into 8-point font with quarter-inch margins. Instead, give your accomplishments - and your recruiter - a chance to breathe!

2. But don't stop there. **Be sure to give the ATS some love, too.** And that means starting with keywords, keywords, and more keywords, straight from the job

description.

3. And finally, when you imagine your poor recruiter
    sweating two great resumes fighting for a single
    interview slot, take all the risk out of the decision by
    making yourself the obvious choice.

So if you're ready to build a resume that obeys these
commandments through and through, just grab a copy right
here: bit.ly/Resume-Google (note that Bitly links are case-
sensitive).

Just click "Make a copy" in Google Docs. Voila, you've got your
perfect resume template ready to rock.

 **Google** Docs

Copy document

Would you like to make a copy of **Google Resume**?

 Make a copy

Wait a second, *what's that you say?*

You were totally with me, right until you saw that the template is two pages long?

And everyone knows that your resume has to be one page, right???

Well funny that you mention that - because someone forgot to tell recruiters about this conventional wisdom.

Specifically, when recruiters in a recent experiment were sent two versions of a resume - 1-page vs. 2-page, they not only preferred the 2 page version, they massively preferred it. And not even just for fancy-pants execs - but even for entry-level candidates.

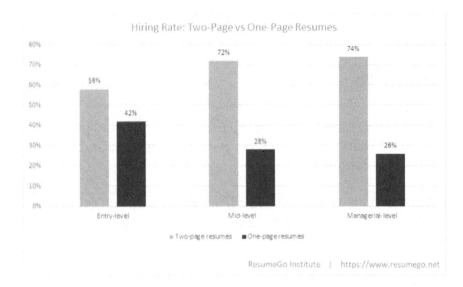

ResumeGo Institute | https://www.resumego.net

Why?

Well, think back to the things that recruiters crave:

- **Making their painful job easier** - for example, looking at a clean resume with a little white space to break up the digital noise.

- **Getting people who have the right keywords and skills** - because they prioritized that over some myth they read about online.

- **And having obvious, rockstar candidates** - i.e., the kinds of candidates who have real experience they can point to and count on.

Well, surprise, surprise - every single one of those things is aided by a 2- page resume.

So bottom line: Use this template. But most importantly, don't accept conventional wisdom when it comes to building an unconventional, rockstar career. Instead, insist on data and proof. Because a great career is too important to leave to chance!

Identify Your Target

Now that you know your audience and you've got the perfect template to serve them, let's get even more specific and focus on a particular job title.

Because, given what you've just learned, why do you think it might be a mistake to apply to multiple kinds of jobs with a single resume?

Is it about the ATS, the recruiter, or even the person the recruiter serves - the hiring manager, AKA your future boss?

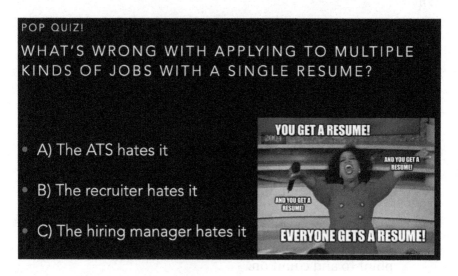

Turns out that it's all of them.

Think of it from each perspective:

- If the **ATS** is looking for Product Manager keywords and your resume is a mishmash of PM, Marketing, and Strategy keywords, you're going to have a much lower match rate than a resume that's 100% dedicated to Product Management keywords.

- If the **Recruiter** is looking for an Obvious Product Manager, why would they want to take a risk on someone who's all over the place on their resume?

- And if the **Hiring Manager** needs someone who can come in and hit the ground running, why would they take a chance on someone who's not even organized enough to be focused on their own CV?

So the bottom line is that you simply have to have a focused resume for each role.

But if you want to apply for multiple roles, fear not - I've got you covered, too.

No matter your preference, head back to your Career Coach GPT Workbook (grab a copy at bit.ly/gptworkbook if you haven't already). This is where you'll do your planning before diving into the resume itself.

And then once you have it open in Google Docs, just click the arrow in the Job Title tab at the bottom to Rename it for your desired job - for instance, Product Manager, Product Marketing Manager, etc. And if you want to go for more than one job, just click Duplicate to create a separate tab.

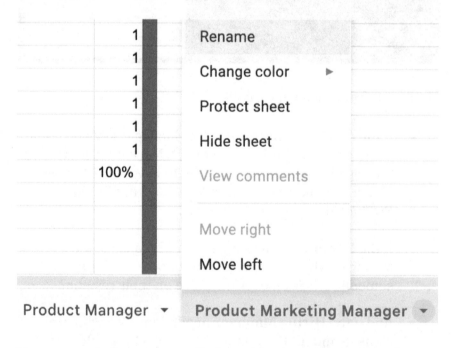

You can apply for as many distinct titles as you want. Just be sure to repeat the following steps for each unique role.

And with that, let's get on to making your first changes directly to the resume itself!

Build Out Your Header

Alright, here we go - time to put digital pen to digital paper. But what do we start with?

Let's go back to that critical question of audience. What do you think recruiters *always* look for right away on your resume?

Is it your name? Your Email Address? Your Job Title?

Well, rather than guess at this critical question, smart researchers have actually done eye tracking studies of real recruiters looking at resumes to find out for sure. And it turns out that almost every time, those recruiter eyes start with job titles.

WHAT'S **THE FIRST THING** A RECRUITER LOOKS FOR AT THE TOP OF YOUR RESUME?

- A) Name

- B) Email

- C) Job Title

Why? Well, as always, go back to those recruiter incentives. If you've got six seconds to figure out whether this candidate is going to get you promoted or fired, do you really care if their email address is JoeSchmoe77@Gmail.com? Nope - you need to know whether they're going to be an obvious candidate or not. And the easiest way to make yourself an obvious candidate is to show that you're in the right space.

So don't overthink it, just start by listing the exact job title at the top of your resume.

Jane Doe
Product Manager

123 Main St. | Anytown, CA 90210
123-456-7890 | email@domain.com

Now I know what you're thinking: What if you're changing careers? For example, let's say you've been a Marketer and now you want to be a Product Manager.

Well, the real question for the recruiter isn't your arbitrary title, but whether you can rock the interview and nail the job. So if you absolutely know that you can be an amazing Product Manager, stand up for the courage of your convictions and lead with that. And then get ready to back it up in every subsequent section we'll cover.

In the meantime, let's talk about winning your other audience: The ATS.

So if you were to look at a real ATS like this one from Greenhouse, one of the things you'd notice is that Location appears prominently in the list of filters.

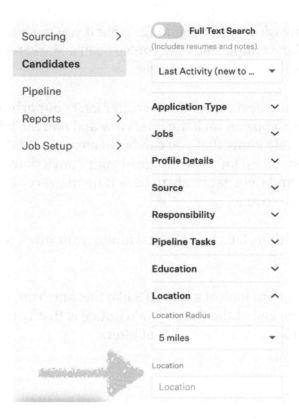

Which makes sense when you go back to the point of an ATS - to help recruiters get through 10,000 resumes as fast as possible. And in this case, that means filtering out candidates who are further away since, all things being equal, a candidate who's local will be easier to close than someone who's on the other side of the country.

Now, of course, in the age of remote work, there are definitely roles where location has no bearing. But even for fully remote roles, there are certain advantages that come with local candidates - you can interview them in- person, you can have them come together for occasional on-sites, and you can even ask them to come back to the office more regularly if the remote work policy ever changes.

So if you are genuinely open to relocation, be sure to signal that on your resume. And the best way to do that is to make yourself a local.

Let's say, for instance, that you're sitting in San Antonio. But all the tech companies you want to work for are based in San Francisco - and that you're considering moving to the Bay Area to pursue some of those roles.

In that case, even if you're reading this steps from the Alamo, it's totally legitimate to list San Francisco on your resume.

Jane Doe
Product Manager

San Francisco, CA
123-4.. /890 | jdoe@gmail.com

That's because:

- Listing San Antonio on your resume might get you automatically filtered out by the ATS, in spite of your future plans.

- If a recruiter asks about your location, you can be 100% honest and explain your intention to move for the right job.

Now, you get the best of both worlds: You can get filtered in by the ATS, but you don't have to make an expensive move until you have the job offer in hand.

Which is the whole point of a great resume, right? Not just to help you get a job, but to give you access to the life you want!

More on that in a bit - but for now, let's get ready for the next critical section: Experience. **Onwards!**

Set Up Your Experience

As you've probably guessed by now, your Experience is critical to both of your key audiences: The Recruiter and the ATS. But because the Experience section is the meatiest part of your resume, some Experience components count more than others.

Let's start with what Recruiters care about - and specifically, what part of your Experience section do they look at the most?

Let's go back to that recruiter eye-tracking study we referenced in the last lesson. We know that recruiters start with job titles at the top of the resume, but when it comes to the Experience section, do they tend to focus on the bullet points, the headings, or the key skills?

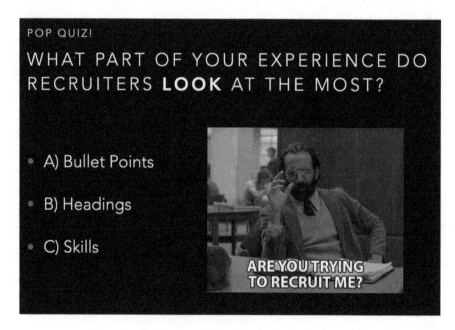

As you might expect for time-starved recruiters, it's all about shortcuts - which means Headings is where they focus. And you can see it for yourself in the following image. There's a consistent pattern that's focused on the top-level view of your career: Where did you work and what did you do? Not: Tell me everything that happened along the way.

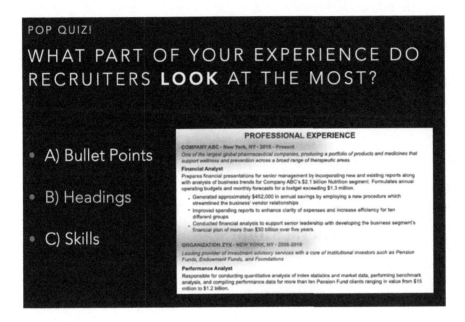

So for now, let's skip the Summary and focus on those critical headings.

Now, one of the biggest mistakes that job-seekers make with their resumes is that they assume it has to be an exhaustive list of everything they've ever done.

So let's be clear about what a resume is and isn't. Just like a job description is a carefully curated ad that promotes the best parts of the job (not every menial task you'll have to do), a resume should be a carefully curated ad that promotes the best parts of your candidacy (not every menial or irrelevant job you've ever done).

In other words, this is not an encyclopedia entry or an IRS tax form. Instead, this is your one small chance to make the case that you belong. Which means that you get to make the call about what gives you the very best case!

And that starts with this simple rule: Include what helps you - *and exclude all the rest.*

Here's an example:

Let's say your resume today starts with your most recent work experience, as well as a leave of absence to take care of a family member with an illness and an earlier summer job.

Experience

General Motors

Ravendale Swimming Pool

Leave of Absence

In that case, start by thinking deeply about what you may be leaving off. For instance, maybe you volunteered as a Project Manager for Habitat for Humanity - but you've left it off because you didn't get paid.

Well again, don't think like a scared job-seeker, think like a time-starved recruiter. If you're hiring for a Project Manager and need to find someone who's going to make you look good, wouldn't you like to know if this candidate has actually done the job before - regardless of compensation?

And sure enough, when I worked at LinkedIn, we polled recruiters on this very question - and 40% said they value Volunteer Experience on par with paid experience. So if you've got awesome volunteer, extracurricular, or entrepreneurial experience, it all belongs in Experience. Period.

Experience

General Motors

Ravendale Swimming Pool

Leave of Absence

Habitat for Humanity

On the other hand, if I'm a recruiter who's moving super fast, how does it help me to know that you used to work at your local pool? Or to know about everything that's happening in your family's life? Instead, it just raises questions about your ability to be organized and concise - the very essence of great project management.

So ditch anything that's irrelevant and focus only on what helps the recruiter choose you.

Experience

General Motors

Habitat for Humanity

Speaking of helping yourself, think carefully about what your dates say about you.

In general Applicant Tracking Systems prefer months and years as shown below, since it's the most common way of listing them. And again, ATS engineers don't waste time training their systems on every random resume template - just the most common ones.

April 2019-Present
Habitat for Humanity

That said, don't forget the human recruiter's own internal algorithm which is that they don't want to bring in a lousy candidate and get fired. And one very quick rule of thumb is that if a candidate doesn't last very long in jobs, it could be a red flag that leads to *their* own demise.

So if you've had to leave jobs after a short duration, even if it wasn't your fault (e.g., you had a lousy boss or lousy timing with layoffs), why give the recruiter an easy excuse to reject you? Instead, convert that short December 2020 to January 2022 stint into year format.

2020-2022

General Motors

Like I said: The resume is *your* story to tell, so don't let anyone else's conventional wisdom dictate how you tell your own story.

And finally, when it comes to storytelling, we all know that details matter. So be sure to include any details that bring your story to life.

This is especially true when you've worked for organizations that aren't household names or in non-standard job titles.

Take this example from Feeding America, an awesome nonprofit that too few people have heard of. The first thing I might do, especially if I were applying into another industry with little nonprofit awareness, is to include a short superlative that will deliver a Halo Effect for me.

April 2019-December 2022

Feeding America (Forbes #1 Top Charity in America)

That way, even if a tech recruiter has never heard of Feeding America, they have heard of Forbes and so knowing that you worked for the leading player in your sector will give them more peace of mind about recommending you.

Similarly, let's say you had a title that was either very specific to the industry you're leaving or totally arbitrary. Anything from Program Fellow to Grand Poobah of Customer Happiness. In that case, it's totally legit to add a slash after your official title with the standard title that's most analogous. For instance, if you were a Program Fellow in the Nonprofit sector but your job was to revamp the website and launch new apps, it would be absolutely fair to also call yourself a Product Manager, since you're actually helping the recruiter understand what you really did at a glance.

April 2019-December 2022
Feeding America (Forbes #1 Top Charity in America) - *Program Fellow / Product Manager*

But just to be clear, it wouldn't be fair at all to call yourself a VP of Sales or Head of Recruiting if those titles had zero bearing on what you did. And when in doubt, just refer to your dream job description. If your job matched the bullets that a recruiter called Business Development or Customer Success, that's 100% fair since you're fully aligned with the recruiter's own language.

And now, with those critical headings filled out for the recruiter, let's move onto the next step, where we'll also give the ATS some love!

Find Your Keywords

With your Experience headings in place, let's start to fill out the bullet points below by understanding what the ATS is looking for. And specifically, think of it this way: If you were an *algorithm*, how would you tell if a candidate was a good fit for a job?

Would you scan the classes they took, the keywords they list, or the GPA they earned?

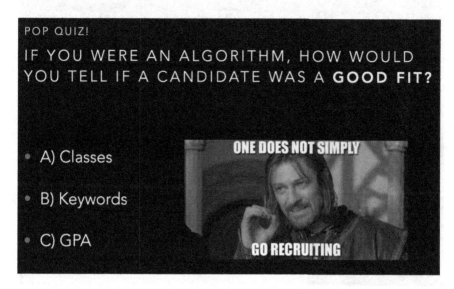

As with all algorithms, you want both *standardized* data and *lots* of it to make a comprehensive judgment - which means that arbitrary class names or a single GPA data point aren't enough. Instead, you want a ton of skills that match the job description - i.e., keywords.

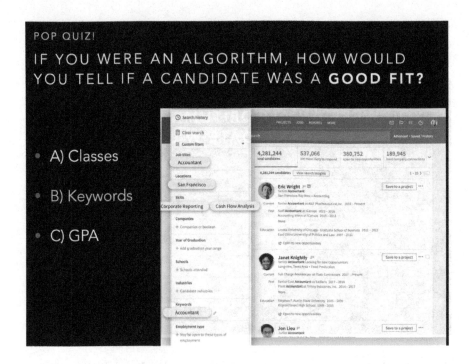

IF YOU WERE AN ALGORITHM, HOW WOULD YOU TELL IF A CANDIDATE WAS A **GOOD FIT?**

- A) Classes

- B) Keywords

- C) GPA

And as you can see here, every single ATS from companies' own systems to LinkedIn's Recruiter platform are basically just keyword crunching machines.

And once they crunch all those keywords, they spit out the one thing the recruiter cares about: Are you an obvious candidate or not?

Specifically, what's your Match Score? Or put another way, how many of the most important keywords from the job description does your resume match?

So, to make sure you end up at the top of this page and not the bottom, where no recruiter will ever actually read your resume, let's start by identifying your most important keywords.

While there are a bunch of paid tools out there to help you do that (e.g., a month of Jobscan costs 5X the price of this book!), I'm going to show you a free and easy hack - using AI, of course.

Here's the prompt:

> *Generate the 20 most important keywords from across ROLE job descriptions.*

 Generate the 20 most important keywords from across Product Manager job descriptions.

 Here are 20 important keywords commonly found in Product Manager job descriptions:

1. Product management
2. Agile methodology
3. Strategy
4. Roadmap
5. Stakeholder management
6. Market research
7. User experience (UX)
8. Data analysis
9. Competitive analysis
10. Product development
11. Cross-functional collaboration

Then, just copy-and-paste those straight into the first column of your Resume Workbook.

Skills
Product management
Agile methodology
Strategy
Roadmap
Stakeholder management
Market research
User experience (UX)
Data analysis
Competitive analysis
Product development
Cross-functional collaboration

And that way you're ready for the big next step: **Building bullets that get you interviews!**

Build Your Bullets

Resume bullets are probably the biggest reason that people hate writing resumes - and also probably the most important source of data for who gets an interview. So it should be no surprise that this delta between importance and anxiety drives a huge number of fatal mistakes.

Now, if you had to guess, which bullet-writing blunder is the most disastrous?

Is it having too many bullets, not listing keywords, or not featuring your achievements?

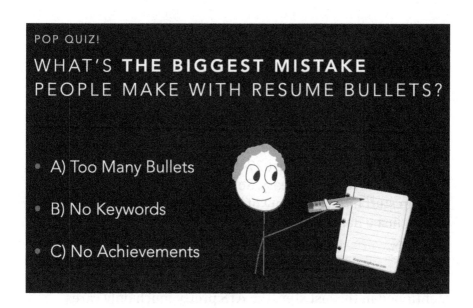

POP QUIZ!

WHAT'S **THE BIGGEST MISTAKE** PEOPLE MAKE WITH RESUME BULLETS?

- A) Too Many Bullets
- B) No Keywords
- C) No Achievements

Well, each of these is so deadly that it's hard to choose just one. So instead, let's understand why each one will get you automatically rejected.

POP QUIZ!

WHAT'S **THE BIGGEST MISTAKE** PEOPLE MAKE WITH RESUME BULLETS?

- A) Too Many Bullets
- B) No Keywords
- C) No Achievements

And to to do that, let's go back to our foundational mandates - The Three Resume Commandments:

1. Make the Recruiter's Job Easy

2. Design Your Resume for Technology

3. Become the Obvious Choice

Let's start with that first one, **making the recruiter's job easy.**
Well, guess what - if you list 27 bullets for every job in 8-point
font, that's anything but easy. So no matter how many keywords
you can stuff into your army of bullet points, keep it lean and
mean - just a handful of the most relevant, compelling bullets
per role.

Next up is not neglecting your other audience: **The ATS.** And as
mentioned in the last step, the ATS pretty much only cares
about keywords. So while building the most poetic, gorgeous
bullets may warm some recruiters' hearts, leaving out critical
keywords from "A/B Testing" to "Zoological Examinations," will
leave the ATS just cold. And your candidacy as well!

Finally, don't forget that recruiters are necessarily **risk-averse.**
They can't put their reputation on the line for a dicey stranger -
they need a slam dunk obvious choice. And so if your resume
has all the right keywords but zero specific achievements, that
leaves the recruiter with zero peace of mind - and on the
lookout for a more obvious candidate.

Thus, to abide by these commandments and sidestep these
pitfalls, let's walk through a fool-proof process for every single
bullet, starting with focus.

Because as mentioned, less is definitely more when it comes to
time-starved recruiters. So start by pulling up your Resume
Workbook and fill up the Job column with three cells for each of
your Experience headings.

Job

Feeding America
Feeding America
Feeding America

Note that each of these rows will eventually represent one bullet for each heading. So yes, that means I'm starting with a limit of three bullets per job. While you can exceed this if necessary, if you follow this process, you'll soon see that extra bullets aren't just optional - they can actually be detrimental. That's because each additional bullet makes the recruiter's job harder - and thus, yours too!

With this skeleton outline set-up, let's now start to put some flesh on those bullet bones in the form of Achievements.

And just to be clear, when I say Achievement, I don't mean what you had to do in the job - i.e., the bullets on your original job description. Because, again, no recruiter wants to put their reputation on the line for someone who just showed up and checked the box. No way, they need awesome candidates, which means they need awesome bullets.

What are Awesome Bullets, you might ask? Well, think of these as the Greatest Hits of your career - the very biggest accomplishments, the most important impact. And to help you generate these, I've got an easy mnemonic for you. Just remember the 3 Ns:

1. **Numbers**
2. **Names**
3. **Notables**

The first is **Numbers**. Again, eye-tracking research shows that we're more likely to pause on a big number than a long string of words. So if there's any way to quantify your work in terms of people reached, time saved, dollars made, or anything else, now's the time to bring out the numerical big guns. As an example, instead of just using the Job Description bullet, "I led website development," focus on what that website actually did - whether it was bringing in more users or more money.

Achievement

New website that generated $1.3M in donations

Next up is **Names**. Because again, eye-tracking science shows that people are more likely to stop for capitalized, famous names than more generic prose. So even if your organization and team wasn't famous, did you partner with or sell to anyone who was?

As mentioned in the last section, the Halo Effect - whereby having your unfamiliar name associated with an established, powerful one starts to earn you some of that credibility - is a powerful one. So instead of just talking about generic partnerships, name names if possible - and ideally household ones that will pop off the page for the recruiter!

Partnership with Google that got 5K volunteers

Finally, we come to **Notables**. While the first two factors may feel somewhat out of your hands (i.e., "Hey Jeremy, how can I blow recruiters away with big numbers and names when I worked for my tiny family-owned business?"), this is one that you can absolutely shape, no matter where you worked. Because unlike Numbers and Names, which are relatively objective, making your achievements notable can be totally subjective.

For instance, let's say your organization launched the 2 millionth app on the App Store. Not very exciting, right? But what if you said you launched the company's very first app. Now, you're rightfully getting credit for your leadership - not getting punished for your context.

Company's first mobile app - 100K installs

So bottom line: Be sure to go well above what your job description listed to make it clear that you're the rockstar obvious candidate every recruiter dreams of. And if you ever feel stuck, go back and look at some of your old performance reviews or ask an old work colleague what they'd list if they were in your shoes. Because we're sometimes our toughest critics, it can be easier to have others point out your awesomeness than to do it all yourself!

And, of course, when in doubt, just turn to our old pal, ChatGPT with the following prompt:

> *What are some example numeric or eye-catching accomplishments that I could list on my resume for X Experience?*

For instance, inserting Project Management will lead to ideas around portfolio size, project completion time, cost-savings, and several other categories!

What are some example numeric or eye-catching accomplishments that I could list on my resume for my Project Manager role?

 Here are some examples of numeric or eye-catching accomplishments that you could list on your resume for a Project Manager role:

1. Successfully managed and delivered a project with a budget of $X, exceeding client expectations and achieving a X% increase in customer satisfaction.
2. Led a cross-functional team of X members to complete a complex project ahead of schedule, resulting in a X% reduction in time-to-market.
3. Implemented project management methodologies resulting in a X% improvement in project efficiency and a X% reduction in costs.
4. Managed X projects simultaneously, ensuring on-time delivery and meeting all project objectives.

And then lastly, when you've got your real, powerful Achievements in place, let's add the final ingredient: **Keywords.**

Because as compelling as achievements are for human recruiters, no recruiter will even see them if your resume doesn't pass the ATS test first. And we know that's all about keywords.

So, with your first three bullet points in place, go back to your list of Skills in the first column and add in the exact Keywords that align with each bullet.

Job	Achievement	Keywords
Feeding America	New website that generated $1.3M in donations	Product Development
Feeding America	Partnership with Google that got 5K volunteers	Strategic Partnership
Feeding America	Company's first mobile app - 100K installs	Product Strategy

Now, I want to be really clear about how Applicant Tracking Systems work:

First, while they sometimes look for variations of keywords - e.g., they might search for both "SaaS" and "Software as a

Service" - you never want to count on this when the outcome is so critical. So please use the exact keyword as it's listed in your Skills column since that represents the most standard usage across millions of profiles.

And second, please don't make the Impostor Syndrome mistake of saying, "Well, we didn't call it X at our company so how can I list it?" For instance, let's say Feeding America described its website work as Platform Optimization. But if you peel back even the first layer on that lexical onion, you'll realize it's basically just Product Development under another name.

So make sure you get credit for as many Keywords as you can - which you can do by adding commas between them and by always using the language of the world you want to enter, not the world you're trying to leave.

Plus, if you get stuck, you can always have ChatGPT pinch-hit for you with a prompt like this:

> Which of the following keywords would be a good fit for my resume based on the following achievements? Please suggest specific relevant keywords from my list for each achievement.
>
> Keywords: PASTE KEYWORDS
>
> Achievements: PASTE ACHIEVEMENTS

Achievement 1: New website that generated $1.3M in donations

Relevant keywords:

* Product management
* Strategy
* User experience (UX)
* Data analysis
* Market research
* Customer insights
* Competitive analysis
* Metrics
* Innovation

And once you've done that, let's put it all together in the form of bullet complete bullet points. Which you can do by leading with your keyword as the action word and then tying it right back to the achievement.

Achievement	Keywords	Bullet Point
New website that generated $1.3M in donations	Product Development	Led product development for new website, leading to $1.3M in new donations
Partnership with Google that got 5K volunteers	Strategic Partnership	Oversaw strategic partnership with Google, generating 5K volunteer applications
Company's first mobile app - 100K installs	Product Strategy	Developed product strategy for the firm's first mobile app, driving 100K installs

Or if writing just isn't your forte, feel free to outsource to ChatGPT with the following prompt:

> *Please combine this achievement and these keywords to make a great resume bullet:*
>
> *Achievement: PASTE ACHIEVEMENT*
>
> *Keywords: PASTE KEYWORDS*

Please combine this achievement and these keywords to make a great resume bullet:

Achievement: New website that generated $1.3M in donations

Keywords: Product management, UX

 Successfully implemented a new website, leveraging strong product management skills and a user-centric approach to optimize user experience (UX), resulting in an impressive $1.3M in donations generated.

And to understand why this approach is so powerful, let's review it against those 3 commandments.

First, having simple and clear bullet points instantly **makes a recruiter's job easy** vs. complex, over-written ones that make them instantly want to give up.

Second, by incorporating keywords into every single bullet, we can make sure that **we'll get past the technology** and onto the human recruiter.

And third, by making every single bullet pop with clear achievements in the form of numbers, names, and notable accomplishments, we take all the risk out of the recruiter's choice, because we are now, at long last, **the obvious choice.**

Finally, to make sure that your bullets are absolutely on-point, be sure to run them through ChatGPT with this prompt:

> *Please rate the following resume bullets based on the impressiveness of their accomplishments and their inclusion of important keywords for X ROLE. And suggest specific ideas to improve them, if possible:*
>
> *BULLET POINTS*

You'll be amazed by how quickly ChatGPT can hone in on these key points - and the improvement ideas it generates.

 Please rate the following resume bullets based on the impressiveness of their accomplishments and their inclusion of important keywords for Product Manager roles. And suggest specific ideas to improve them, if possible:

-Led product development for new website, leading to $1.3M in donations

 The provided resume bullet is impressive in terms of showcasing the accomplishment of leading product development for a new website and resulting in $1.3M in donations. However, it can be further improved by including additional keywords and providing more context. Here's a revised version:

* Successfully led end-to-end product development and launch of a new website, driving a record-breaking $1.3M in donations within [specific time frame].

Improvement suggestions:

* Specify the timeline within which the $1.3M in donations was achieved to provide more context and demonstrate the speed of impact.
* Consider incorporating relevant keywords such as "user engagement," "conversion optimization," or "fundraising strategy" to highlight additional skills and areas of expertise.

Now I know you may be thinking: "Jeremy, I can come up with three awesome bullets with ChatGPT, no problem. And I'll even cover some of the most important skills. But there's just no way I can credibly cover *every* skill. So why bother applying, right?"

Wrong.

Because, even if you look over at your Skills column and see that you're only partly qualified, it turns out that not even recruiters want you to be 100% qualified.

Sure enough, in that study that TalentWorks ran a few years back, your best chance of getting an interview was being about 50% qualified on your resume - not 100%.

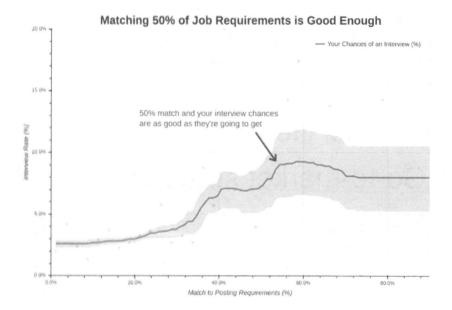

Matching 50% of Job Requirements is Good Enough

— Your Chances of an Interview (%)

50% match and your interview chances
are as good as they're going to get

Interview Rate (%)

Match to Posting Requirements (%)

Why is that?

Well, again, remember that recruiters are savvy professionals just like you who know they need to hire someone *fast*. So if they only go after people who are 100% qualified, those folks are less likely to accept their interview offers - and even their job offers. After all, why bother going through all the hassle of leaving your current company just to do the exact same job you can already do in your sleep?

So recruiters have found that candidates who are 50% qualified are the perfect balance of being able to do the job - but also have the hunger to switch companies and come in with guns blazing. In other words, the truly obvious candidates that will get them promoted! ⚡

So before you give up in desperation, just do this last check: See if you can find a few more keywords that can bump you closer to that magic 50% mark.

Cool Feature Alert!
If you use the exact keywords listed under the Skills column of your workbook, you'll get a real-time tally of your match rate right in the lower left-hand corner:

Product lifecycle	1
Go-to-market strategy	1
Metrics	0
Innovation	0
Stakeholder manageme	0
Strategy	0
% Qualified	40%

For instance, if you're already leading with a great keyword at the start of your bullet, maybe there's a chance to include keywords at the middle or the end. If you do you may discover your qualification rate shooting up, right into the target zone.

Keywords	Bullet Point
Product Strategy, Mobile Application, Analytics	Developed product strategy for the firm's first mobile application, driving go-to-market strategy and analytics that led to 100K installs

Or even just flat-out ask ChatGPT to find the Venn Diagram overlap between what you did and the keyword you want to incorporate, like so:

Suggest a revision of this resume bullet to incorporate KEYWORDS:

RESUME BULLET

 Suggest a revision of this resume bullet to incorporate "mobile application" and "analytics":

-Led product development for new website, leading to $1.3M in donations

 • Successfully led end-to-end product development and launch of a mobile application and website, resulting in a record-breaking $1.3M in donations. Utilized analytics to optimize user engagement, conversion rates, and fundraising strategy within [specific time frame].

And when you get to that magic mark of ~50%, you'll know that it's time to move on to the next section: **Education.**

Add Your Education

OK, we've just spent the last three steps focused on Experience, so you might feel like you could use a breather when it comes to Education.

With that in mind, what do you think is the biggest difference between Experience and Education?

Maybe the ATS doesn't scan your Education section? Or recruiters don't care about it? Or maybe it just doesn't matter, period???

POP QUIZ!

WHAT'S **THE BIGGEST DIFFERENCE** BETWEEN
YOUR EDUCATION AND EXPERIENCE SECTIONS?

- A) Education Isn't Scanned

- B) Recruiters Don't Read It

- C) It Doesn't Matter

I think you'll find that what we lack in formal education, we more than make up for in street smarts.

Well, if you happened to guess any of those, you'd be wrong.

Because it turns out Education is important enough to be hard-wired right into the ATS - and the recruiters' brains.

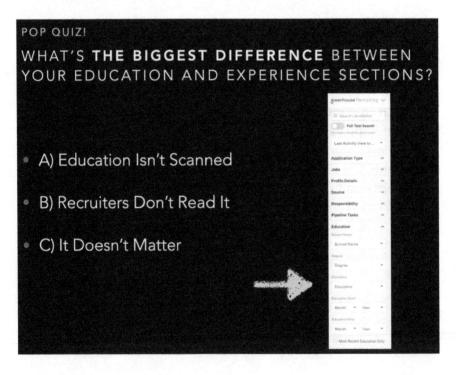

POP QUIZ!

WHAT'S **THE BIGGEST DIFFERENCE** BETWEEN
YOUR EDUCATION AND EXPERIENCE SECTIONS?

- A) Education Isn't Scanned

- B) Recruiters Don't Read It

- C) It Doesn't Matter

To understand how that wiring works, let's start with the ATS.

Because the ATS has been trained to understand the most common resume formats, it starts by looking for all the key components of a traditional Education section: *School, Degree, Discipline,* and *Dates.*

Which means you should start by nailing each of these items in your headers, in turn.

Education

June 2015-July 2016
General Assembly - *Product Management Certificate*

September 2010-May 2012
University of Washington - *MA, Education*

September 1999-May 2003
Penn State University - *BA, Philosophy*

Note: Even if you didn't go to a traditional school (e.g., maybe you earned a certificate like in the above example), at least include as much of this information as possible since it all gets scanned by the ATS.

And then, don't stop here - which is where way too many candidates stop. Instead, remember that bullet points always matter, no matter where they appear on the resume. And so not only do you want to include bullet points under Education, you want to make sure they all abide by your Three Resume Commandments:

1. Make the Recruiter's Job Easy

2. Design Your Resume for Technology

3. Become the Obvious Choice

That means start by making the recruiter's job **easy**. So instead of giving them no education bullets or a dozen, just give them 1–2 highly relevant ones per experience. You can set it up in your Resume Workbook like so:

Experience

General Assembly

University of Washington

Penn State University

And just because these are educational experiences, don't think for a second that they're exempt from the requirements of the **ATS**. So be sure to think broadly about any of your most important keywords to include.

Keywords

User Experience

Cross-functional Team

Business Development

Finally, make yourself **obvious**. Which means finding a real achievement lurking behind every experience and bullet point.

Achievement

App won first place in the App Accelerator contest

Organized first-ever EdTech Club for 150 students

Launched campus startup that reached 25K students

And should you ever find yourself stuck on your Education section, try this exercise: Don't just think about academic achievements. Instead, think about the most important things you did during school, period. It could be a club, a volunteer project, or even a student venture. Whatever made the biggest impact in both your life and the lives of others during this time is likely what a recruiter really wants to hear about, not just the random things you had to do to graduate.

Or even ask ChatGPT for a little nudge:

> *What experiences from my EDUCATION might be relevant for an X role?*

 What experiences from my undergraduate degree might be relevant for a Product Manager role?

 An undergraduate degree offers a wide range of experiences that can be relevant for a Product Manager role. Here are some key experiences that may be valuable:

1. Coursework in Business or Marketing: Courses in business administration, marketing, or related fields can provide a foundational understanding of marketing principles, market analysis, consumer behavior, and strategic planning. This knowledge is beneficial for developing effective product strategies and positioning.
2. Group Projects and Collaboration: Many undergraduate programs involve group projects, which develop teamwork, collaboration, and communication skills. These experiences are valuable for a Product Manager who needs to work closely with cross-functional teams, stakeholders, and developers to drive successful product outcomes.
3. Research and Data Analysis: Undertaking research projects and analyzing data during your undergraduate studies can help you develop skills in gathering, interpreting, and drawing insights from information. These skills are crucial for conducting market research, analyzing user feedback, and making data-driven product decisions.

Then, when you've got all your resume ingredients ready, use the Keyword + Achievement formula to put them together into powerful Bullet Points:

Experience	Achievement	Keywords	Bullet Point
General Assembly	App won first place in the App Accelerator contest	User Experience	App won first place in GA's App Accelerator contest; also earned a special prize for Top User Experience
University of Washington	Organized first-ever EdTech Club for 150 students	Cross-functional Team	Led cross-functional team to organize UW's first-ever EdTech Club, reaching 150 students
Penn State University	Launched campus startup that reached 25K students	Business Development	Launched campus startup that reached 25K students; served as the business development lead and closed deals with 10 area businesses

And lastly, be sure to run them through that same ChatGPT prompt from the last section to see if you've left anything on the table.

Please rate the following resume bullets based on the impressiveness of their accomplishments and their inclusion of important keywords for X ROLE. And suggest specific ideas to improve them, if possible:

BULLET POINTS

Please rate the following resume bullets based on the impressiveness of their accomplishments and their inclusion of important keywords for Product Manager roles. And suggest specific ideas to improve them, if possible:

-Launched campus startup that reached 25K students; served as the business development lead and closed deals with 10 area businesses

The provided resume bullets are impressive in terms of launching a campus startup, reaching 25K students, and closing deals with area businesses. They also include important keywords such as "business development" and "deals." Here is the rating and improvement suggestion:

1. Launched campus startup that reached 25K students; served as the business development lead and closed deals with 10 area businesses.

Rating: 4/5

Improvement suggestion:

* Specify the nature or industry of the campus startup to provide more context and demonstrate your expertise in a particular field.

And now, with our Experience and Education sections complete, we're heading into the homestretch of the resume all of a sudden. So keep that momentum going as we roll into Skills next!

List Your Skills

Sitting at the bottom of your resume, the Skills section can often feel like a throwaway. And yet, it's a final chance to remedy one of the biggest blunders that sinks job-seekers.

To understand why, let's start with this question: What percentage of job- seekers do you think believe they're clearly communicating their skills on their resumes?

Is it as low as 42%, as high as 79%, or somewhere in between?

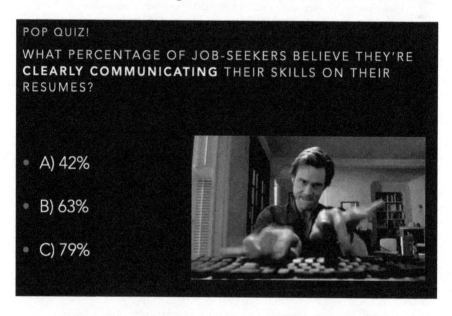

POP QUIZ!

WHAT PERCENTAGE OF JOB-SEEKERS BELIEVE THEY'RE **CLEARLY COMMUNICATING** THEIR SKILLS ON THEIR RESUMES?

- A) 42%

- B) 63%

- C) 79%

Well, it turns out that nearly 4 in 5 of us are confident that we're nailing one of the most critical tasks.

WHAT PERCENTAGE OF JOB-SEEKERS BELIEVE THEY'RE
CLEARLY COMMUNICATING THEIR SKILLS ON THEIR
RESUMES?

- A) 42%

- B) 63%

- C) 79%

"A survey by CareerBuilder found that **79%** of job seekers believe they clearly communicate their skills on their resumes."

But now let's flip that question on its head: What percentage of recruiters feel the same way about the resumes they're seeing?

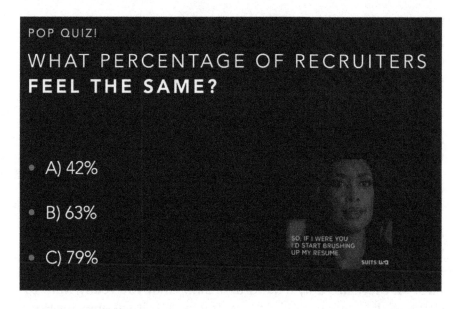

POP QUIZ!

WHAT PERCENTAGE OF RECRUITERS FEEL THE SAME?

- A) 42%

- B) 63%

- C) 79%

SO, IF I WERE YOU
I'D START BRUSHING
UP MY RESUME

SUITS ᴜ·ᑫ

And as you might expect, that percentage is nearly half the rate of the jobseekers' confident take.

POP QUIZ!

WHAT PERCENTAGE OF RECRUITERS FEEL THE SAME?

- A) 42%

- B) 63%

- C) 79%

"According to a study by the Society for Human Resource Management (SHRM), just **42%** of employers feel that job candidates are effectively conveying their skills on their resumes."

What accounts for this discrepancy?

Well, even if an ATS can instantaneously pull out all of our skills buried deep within bullet points, our frail human brains aren't quite as capable. Especially when you consider that six seconds per resume only allows for a cursory scan - not a deep read.

So to close this gap and make the recruiters' job easier, why not just spell out your most critical skills where even a busy recruiter can't miss them?

Enter the Skills section!

And there are two ways you can make that section work for you:

First - if there are only a handful of skills that you really want to emphasize because they're by far the most critical ones for the role, you can give each one its own bullet - complete with impressive achievements.

Skills

- **Product**
  - *SaaS:* Consulted for a SaaS business during grad school, helped it achieve $100K ARR
  - *Agile Methodologies:* Leveraged Agile to run EdTech Club efficiently
  - *Business Strategy:* Developed business strategy for a local small business, earning a $200K loan from the SBA

And the advantage here over the Experience and Education bullets is that because you're highlighting the key skill at the start of the bullet, it will really pop for recruiters - not just the ATS.

Or second, if you've got a ton of important skills to cover, you can just list them out as shown here. Just be sure to remember the poor, frazzled recruiter who's frantically scanning your resume - and make their job easier by using categories to help them understand which larger areas you're covering.

Skills

- *Product:* SaaS, Agile Methodologies, Business Strategy, Product Marketing, Product Design
- *Tech:* SQL, HTML/CSS, Google Analytics, AdWords, Retargeting, Salesforce

Plus, if you like that technique, here's a handy little prompt to make it easy:

Place these skills into categories: PASTE IN SKILLS LIST

Place these skills into categories: Product management, Agile methodology, Strategy, Roadmap, Stakeholder management, Market research, User experience (UX), Data analysis, Competitive analysis, Product development, Cross-functional collaboration, Prioritization, Requirements gathering, Metrics, Project management, Innovation, User feedback, Problem-solving, Product lifecycle, Go-to-market strategy

 Based on the provided skills, here is a categorized breakdown:

Product Management:

* Product management
* Roadmap
* Stakeholder management
* Product development
* Prioritization
* Requirements gathering
* Product lifecycle

Agile and Project Management:

* Agile methodology
* Project management

And lest you feel like you're forgetting the ATS here, keep in mind that this technology not only looks for keywords *matches* but also keyword *density*. In other words, someone who has multiple mentions of a keyword may get a higher match score than someone who only mentions it once. So don't hesitate to incorporate your most important terms a few times!

And now that we've reached the bottom of your resume, let's bounce back to the top to finish off the Summary section in the next lesson.

Complete Your Summary

I know, I know - it's so tempting to just be done with your resume after all these steps. Why bother with a summary at all?

Well, the one cardinal rule we've embraced from the very beginning is that we always have to be honest about who our audience is and what they care about.

So here's one last resume pop quiz before we move on to cover letters: What do you think the Top Third rule is?

A. 1/3 of candidates get interviewed

B. Recruiters read the top 1/3 of your resume

C. The ATS looks for 1/3 of the top keywords

Now, as you may recall from the very first pop quiz, A is way off - only about 1–2% of applicants get interviewed. Which is why a great resume is so important in the first place.

And if you've been paying attention to our deep dive into ATS technology, you know that the power of this technology is that it scans for everything - not just the handful of things our human minds can pick out.

So by pure process of elimination, the answer is, indeed, B.

But that also should make sense on its own. After all, if you were a busy recruiter with 6 seconds to spend on a resume, would you want to read the whole thing if the first part sucked?

No way.

And sure enough, as you can see from this Executive Recruiter's quote, the Top Third Rule is all about using the beginning of the resume to test whether the rest is worthwhile:

> *"Recruiters scan the top third of each resume and decide almost instantly whether the applicant could be a potential fit. If the top third shows*

promise, the recruiter will invest more time with the rest of the resume's details. If the top third doesn't jump out, however, the recruiter moves on."

-HfH Executive Search Partners

So to make sure your resume passes this test, let's return one last time to our three commandments, starting with #1 - **making the recruiter's job easier.**

And because a recruiter isn't an all-devouring algorithm, you don't want to overwhelm them in the very first second with a random job experience or a completely abstract objective.

Instead, give them exactly what they need to know: One tight, perfect sentence that says *"I'm the candidate you're looking for."*

And how do you do that? Basically just reverse engineer the first sentence of the job description.

For instance, let's say the job description says they're looking for a product manager who can launch awesome products that produce a social impact:

Code for America is looking for a talented Product Manager who can launch products that deliver significant social impact for our communities.

Well, guess what? The first line of your Summary is practically written already:

Summary

Product manager with a track record of successful launches in the social impact space:

And then, because we're still trying to balance between the needs of the recruiter and the ATS, let's also give a little love to our **technological friend.**

So once again, let's go back to the job description - but this time, let's focus on the keywords:

Product Manager
Code for America · San Francisco, CA (Remote)

<u>In This Position You Will</u>
- Own the product strategy and execution of a program or program area
- Help lead a multi-disciplinary team of design, research, and engineering to test and develop new solutions that work for underserved communities and grow our overall client base
- Participate in research and interactions with users: understanding what we're trying to learn and why and ensuring the right outcomes from research

With these in hand, let's back up your bold first sentence by tying it to the three most critical skills:

Summary

Product manager with a track record of successful launches in the social impact space:

- *Product Strategy:*
- *Multi-Disciplinary Leadership:*
- *Research:*

And finally, get ready to ace the Top Third Test by not just sounding good in theory, but by becoming **obvious** out there where it matters - in Achievement Land.

And the best way to become obvious is to lead with the three most impressive accomplishments from across your resume that will make the recruiter feel like they're well on their way to a promotion:

Summary

Product manager with a track record of successful launches in the social impact space:

- *Product Strategy:* Established strategy for new Feeding America website that generated $1.3M in incremental donations
- *Multi-Disciplinary Leadership:* Worked with a cross-functional team of designers, engineers, and data scientists to launch a leading nonprofit's very first app
- *Research:* Led UX research sessions with prospective users across the country, leading to 100K app downloads within the first month of launch

Now, I know you might be nervous: "Wait a second, Jeremy, aren't these the same bullets from down below?" But remember the implication of the Top Third Rule: Just like no human recruiter will ever read your resume unless it passes the ATS Test, no recruiter will ever read the bottom of your resume unless the top passes the Top Third Test.

So even at the risk of duplication, always, always, always lead with your best stuff so that you can make it to the next phase. And then just remember that the ATS loves to see keyword density, so you're still doing yourself a big favor algorithmically.

Finally, make sure that your summary is in tip-top shape by testing it with the following ChatGPT prompt:

Please rate the following resume summary based on how clear my interest is in a X role and how impressive and relevant my accomplishments are. And suggest specific ideas to improve it, if possible:

INSERT SUMMARY

Please rate the following resume summary based on how clear my interest is in a Product Manager role and how impressive and relevant my accomplishments are. And suggest specific ideas to improve it, if possible:

Product manager with a track record of successful launches in the social impact space:
• Product Strategy: Established strategy for new Feeding America website that generated $1.3M in incremental donations
• Multi-Disciplinary Leadership: Worked with a cross-functional team of designers, engineers, and data scientists to launch a leading nonprofit's very first app
• Research: Led UX research sessions with prospective users across the country, leading to 100K app downloads within the first month of launch

The provided resume summary demonstrates a clear interest in a Product Manager role and includes impressive and relevant accomplishments. Here's the rating and improvement suggestion:

Rating: 4.5/5

Improvement suggestion:

* The resume summary is already quite strong. However, to make it even more impactful, consider incorporating specific quantifiable metrics or percentages for the accomplishments mentioned.

And with that done, your resume is now fully optimized from top to bottom and across your two essential audiences. So download it as a PDF to preserve the formatting for the human recruiter while still making it easy for the ATS to read - and then get ready for the rubber to hit the road. Because it's **application time!** ⚡

4) Find + Apply on Autopilot

With your resume in hand, let's not waste a second getting it out to the world - and getting it the attention it deserves!

So we'll cover three steps in this chapter:

1. Finding jobs

2. Applying with a personalized cover letter

3. Getting a referral

How to Find the Best Jobs Automatically

The first thing you need to know about job applications is that timing is just as important as quality. That's because recruiters vastly prefer applications in the first few days after a job is posted versus ones that come in weeks later.

Why?

Think of a new job post like Christmas morning. It's this magical moment when everything feels fresh and new. You can't wait to rush downstairs to see the tree and open your presents. And that's exactly how a recruiter feels about the first few applicants - every resume is full of possibility!

Now think of the week after Christmas. There's still shreds of wrapping paper lying around, the tree is starting to tilt to one side, and everyone is absolutely sick of eggnog. That's exactly what the 127th applicant feels like to recruiters - no matter how great their resume.

Which is why it's no surprise that a TalentWorks study found that applicants in the first 96 hours after a job posting were up to 8X more likely to land interviews than those who applied later:

When Should You Apply for a Job?

And which is why it's so critical to be an early applicant.

Thus, to make sure that you get your foot in the door early, just do the following:

1) Set-up job alerts for your specific job title on all your preferred job boards - including both the big ones (LinkedIn, Indeed) and the specialty ones (e.g., Wellfound for startup jobs, Idealist for nonprofit jobs). And if you want to make sure you're being thorough, feel free to search a couple of related titles based on this ChatGPT prompt:

> *What are the most common other job titles companies use instead of ROLE?*

What are the most common other job titles companies use instead of Sales?

"Sales" is a widely recognized job title, but there are several alternative job titles that companies may use to refer to similar roles within their organizations. Here are some of the most common alternative job titles used instead of "Sales":

1. Account Executive
2. Business Development Representative (BDR)
3. Sales Representative
4. Sales Consultant
5. Sales Associate

2) Set aside an hour each day to review these alerts.

3) For every job you're even remotely interested in, apply that same day.

Not only will this strategy boost your odds for the reasons discussed above, but applying broadly has two side benefits:

A) We humans are notoriously lousy about being able to predict what will make us happy. And that's especially true when it comes to careers. As an example, I once landed a job at Google - only to quit six weeks later because it made me so miserable! Thus, because a single job description is a frail canvas to evaluate our future happiness on, it's best to cast your net widely and discover more about jobs over time as you get to meet the real people behind them.

B) Even if a certain job turns out to be less-than-enticing during the interview phase, just having a few suitors in your back pocket can make all the difference for the job you really do want. Going back to that Google example, when I was still applying, my recruiter warned me that it often took several months to earn an offer. But then when I informed him that I had an offer in hand from a competitor (albeit one that I wasn't excited about), I got my Google offer the following week. Which just goes to show that even the mightiest employers aren't immune to the leverage that competition gives you!

So bottom line: Apply early and often! :)

How to Get the Best of Both Cover Letter Worlds

But wait a second. I totally skipped over that age-old question that's frustrated so many job seekers: *To write a cover letter or not?*

Well, just like every other controversial question we've tackled so far, surely this one can be solved with data.

Like, do recruiters even read cover letters or not?

And sure enough there's been a ton of research on this question. The only problem is that it's not conclusive.

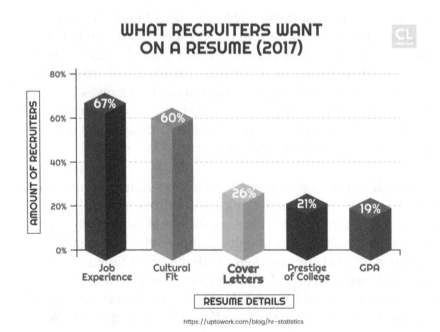

WHAT RECRUITERS WANT ON A RESUME (2017)

https://uptowork.com/blog/hr-statistics

That's because unlike an ATS that follows the same rules for every company and every job, every recruiter has their own, highly personal rules of thumb.

So you end up with mixed results like this because some recruiters never read cover letters and some always do. But you never know *which one is which* until it's too late.

So what's a stressed-out job-seeker to do? Well, just like we challenge conventional wisdom with data, let's tackle ambiguity through the power of flowcharts!

That's right, here's a simple heuristic to help you decide when to write and when to save your time for more important activities.

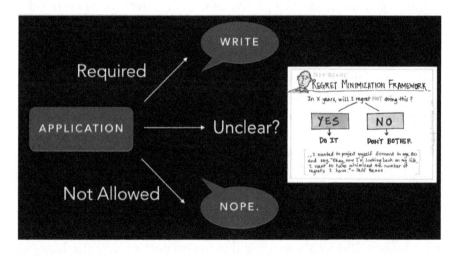

Let's start with the job application itself. Happily, a small percentage of caring recruiters will save your sanity by either requiring a cover letter or forbidding it.

So no need to overthink these situations - as a general rule, nothing irks recruiters more when candidates can't follow instructions, so just go with the flow.

But what about those 90% of applications that just aren't clear?

In those cases, let's steal a framework from Jeff Bezos, who had to tackle tons of ambiguity when he was building the first online bookstore.

Specifically, think about where a given job falls in your own career and life trajectory. If it's a potential life-changer and you're going to be on your deathbed someday, ruing the fact that you didn't give this application every last shot, by all means write a cover letter. Even if it's never read, you won't have to lose a wink of sleep for the rest of your life wondering what could have been...

On the other hand, let's be real: Some jobs may get your heart fluttering while there are plenty of others where you just need the money or the health insurance or whatever to get you to the next job that really will change your life. If the job in question is that kind of job, I hereby give you permission to skip the cover letter. Sure, there's a small but not impossible chance that the cover letter could have gotten you an interview. But the great thing about So-What Jobs like these is that there are lots of them out there. So you don't have to worry about minimizing regrets when you wouldn't have had them to begin with!

Now, with that all resolved, assuming you do have to write a cover letter - either because it's required by the recruiter or your future conscience - let's cover exactly how to do that in the next lesson. But as always, we'll focus on getting you the biggest impact with the least effort, so even if you're running on application fumes at this point, just know that the finish line is in sight!

Write a Pareto Cover Letter

OK, with our last bit of application energy, let's write a cover letter that lands you interviews. But not just any cover letter - a Pareto Cover Letter.

To explain what I mean, consider this question: What's the biggest mistake people make with cover letters?

Is it about deviating from the standard cover letter template, not using the right format, or maybe not submitting a full-length letter?

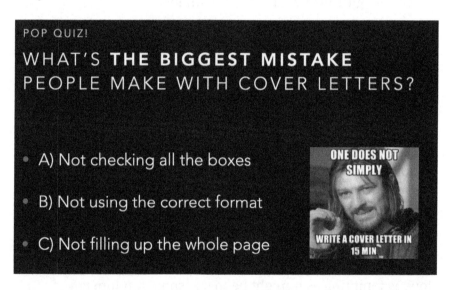

While I know that I used to freak out about all of these things, here's the only thing I worry about now after having reviewed thousands of cover letters from other job-seekers: Does my cover letter respect the *Pareto Principle?*

For those who haven't heard the term before, this is just another name for the classic 80/20 rule.

In other words, 80% of the things we think are important - things like templates, formats, blah, blah, blah - end up being completely unimportant. And only 20% of what we do ultimately drives the vast majority of our results.

Now, the trick, of course, is that we often don't know what's the important 20% or the unimportant 80% before we begin. So let me give you a big clue for cover letters: It's all about the Three Commandments.

1. Make the Recruiter's Job Easy

2. Design Your Resume for Technology

3. Become the Obvious Choice

Because, believe it or not, cover letters are governed by the exact same rules as resumes. That's because when a recruiter reviews your cover letter or an ATS scans your letter, they don't differentiate between it and your resume. Instead, they're still focused on the same things as always - do I understand this person, do they match the role, and are they going to get me fired or promoted?

So let's go right back to the first commandment: **Making the recruiters' job easy.**

Now, as tempting as it might be to use some random cover letter template from Microsoft Word or that you found on the internet, starting with letterhead, the recruiter's own address, and a super wordy opening paragraph does nothing to help your friend, the recruiter. On the contrary, it just makes their lives more tedious and painful. So do them a solid and just cut to the chase. Specifically, start by addressing the biggest and really, the only question: Why should they hire you?

I'm thrilled by the opportunity to apply for this role for two reasons:

And then don't just talk the talk, be sure to walk it, too.

Because surprise, surprise, many **Applicant Tracking Systems** can scan your cover letter as well as your resume. And we all know by now that the ATS couldn't care less about talk - all it wants is keywords.

Which keywords you ask? The same ones we've been focused on all along, of course - the ones straight out of job descriptions:

Product Manager
Code for America · San Francisco, CA (Remote)

Apply ☑   Save   · · ·

In This Position You Will
- Own the product strategy and execution of a program or program area
- Help lead a multi-disciplinary team of design, research, and engineering to test and develop new solutions that work for underserved communities and grow our overall client base
- Participate in research and interactions with users: understanding what we're trying to learn and why and ensuring the right outcomes from research

.

And so your first big rationale for the job should be a keyword tour de force, covering all the skills and expertise you'll bring to the role - and that will light up your ATS match score at the same time!

I'm thrilled by the opportunity to apply for this role for two reasons:

1) I'm obsessed with world-class product development. From leading product strategy for a multi-disciplinary team at Feeding America to driving research with users across the country, I love nothing more than learning from people and turning those insights into a product that customers fall in love with.

And then, to close strong, give the recruiter the assurance they need that you're the obvious candidate they've been seeking.

Don't just say "Hey - I'm a generic candidate for these kinds of roles." Instead, let them know that you've got a specific passion for their role in particular. So that way, they can visualize you walking into the interview room and knocking the hiring manager's socks off.

I'm thrilled by the opportunity to apply for this role for two reasons:

1) I'm obsessed with world-class product development. From leading product strategy for a multi-disciplinary team at Feeding America to driving research with users across the country, I love nothing more than learning from people and turning those insights into a product that customers fall in love with.

2) And I'm deeply passionate about Code for America's mission. Empowering organizations to serve their communities is something that's motivated me throughout my life - from starting UW's first EdTech Club to bringing Feeding America to the hungry across the US. And by bringing incredible technical expertise into our local governments, CFA is very much pushing the envelope of what's possible for the next generation of civil servants.

Thus, between being energized by the day-to-day work and the overall mission, I can't imagine a better opportunity to apply my product management skills in the name of something truly meaningful!

And if they can visualize that, they can already visualize their raise hitting their checking account. Which means they're already moving you into the interview queue...

So like I said: The cover letter isn't a whole new system to master. It's the exact same audience and the exact same incentives. So don't waste a second checking boxes or filling out fluff. Just head over to this link to grab my short and focused template: bit.ly/yourcltemplate

And then, tap into the power of ChatGPT to make sure your cover letter is awesome in two ways:

1) Test that it's working for your audiences with this prompt:

Please rate the following cover letter for an X role based on how clearly my skills and passion align with the role. And suggest specific ideas to improve it, if possible:

INSERT COVER LETTER

 Rating: 4/5

The provided cover letter effectively showcases your skills and passion aligning with the Product Manager role. Here's an improvement suggestion:

* Start the cover letter with a strong introductory sentence that immediately grabs the reader's attention and highlights your enthusiasm. For example: "I am thrilled to apply for the Product Manager role as it combines my passion for world-class product development with my deep commitment to Code for America's mission."
* In the first reason, mention specific achievements or results from your experience at Feeding America and working with users to showcase your impact and skills in product development.
* In the second reason, provide more specific examples of how you have empowered organizations and brought about positive change through your involvement with UW's first EdTech Club and Feeding America. Emphasize the direct connection between your previous experiences and Code for America's mission.

Now, you can feel confident that your cover letter is ready for primetime. But since you know that a great cover letter should be personalized to a specific company and role, here's how to quickly create multiple versions:

2) To update the second paragraph for each company as fast as possible, try this prompt:

Rewrite the following cover letter paragraph to focus on X EMPLOYER:

INSERT PARAGRAPH

Rewrite the following cover letter paragraph to focus on Google:
2) And I'm deeply passionate about Code for America's mission. Empowering organizations to serve their communities is something that's motivated me throughout my life - from starting UW's first EdTech Club to bringing Feeding America to the hungry across the US. And by bringing incredible technical expertise into our local governments, CFA is very much pushing the envelope of what's possible for the next generation of civil servants.

 2. And I'm deeply passionate about Google's mission. Empowering individuals and organizations through technology has been a driving force in my life. From starting UW's first EdTech Club to leveraging digital solutions at Feeding America to combat hunger across the US, I have witnessed firsthand the transformative power of technology. Google, with its cutting-edge innovation and global reach, has continuously pushed the boundaries of what's possible, and I am excited to contribute my skills and passion to further advance the next generation of groundbreaking products and services.

And now you have a cover letter generation system that should only take you about 5 minutes per application. Which means more time for the next, even more important step...

How to Get Your Foot in the Door

So clearly, when you apply and what you apply with are essential to your success. But it turns out that *how* you apply is even more important!

If you had to guess, which of these three application channels gives you the best odds of getting an interview:

A) Applying on a company's website

B) Applying via an online job board

C) Applying via a referral from a current employee

If you guessed "C," you're absolutely right. But did you know that it's not a 10% boost to your chances? Or even a 100% boost? But a 1,000% boost.

Let me just let that sink in for a second.

According to data gathered on millions of job-seekers across dozens of industries, you are 10X more likely to land an interview just by getting a referral.

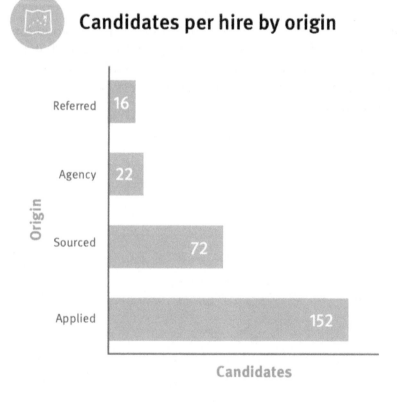

Candidates per hire by origin

Why is that?

Well put yourself back in the recruiter's shoes. If you're receiving hundreds of applications for every job, do you really want to read all those resumes? Or put your reputation on the line for a stranger you've never met?

Heck no.

You want a sure thing.

And what's the surest, safest bet?

Going with a referral - i.e., the wisdom of someone you already know and trust.

Plus, it turns out that referred candidates aren't just good for the recruiter - they're great for the organization, too. That's because other studies show that referred candidates are more likely to show up for interviews, accept offers, and stay longer at the companies

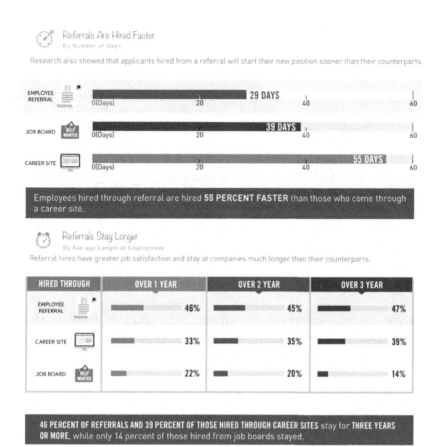

Referrals Are Hired Faster
By Number of Days

Research also showed that applicants hired from a referral will start their new position sooner than their counterparts.

	0(Days)	20	40	60
EMPLOYEE REFERRAL		**29 DAYS**		
JOB BOARD		**39 DAYS**		
CAREER SITE			**55 DAYS**	

Employees hired through referral are hired **55 PERCENT FASTER** than those who come through a career site.

Referrals Stay Longer
By Average Length of Employment

Referral hires have greater job satisfaction and stay at companies much longer than their counterparts.

HIRED THROUGH	OVER 1 YEAR	OVER 2 YEAR	OVER 3 YEAR
EMPLOYEE REFERRAL	46%	45%	47%
CAREER SITE	33%	35%	39%
JOB BOARD	22%	20%	14%

46 PERCENT OF REFERRALS AND 39 PERCENT OF THOSE HIRED THROUGH CAREER SITES stay for THREE YEARS OR MORE, while only 14 percent of those hired from job boards stayed.

Which is why referrals are treated like gold inside pretty much every organization - **and why you need a referral.**

How to Get a Referral

While getting a referral may seem like a daunting task, especially if you're switching to a new career path, it really just boils down to a simple Venn diagram:

Can you find someone who both can help you (i.e., they work at your desired company) and wants to help you (i.e., they have something in common with you)?

Let's start with the left side of that diagram: Who's even in a position to help you in the first place?

To find out, just follow these two steps:

1) After you've applied for a job in that crucial 96-hour window, search for and open the employer's Company Page on LinkedIn:

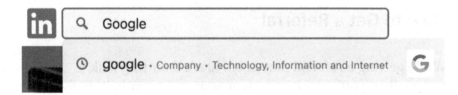

2) Click on the number of employees:

for
everyone

Google

Technology, Information and Internet · Mountain View, CA · 28,817,659 followers

 Ranked on LinkedIn Top Companies

 Miguel & 389 other connections work here · 280,991 employees ⬅

(✓ Following) (**Visit website** ℃) (More)

Voila! You now have a company directory that's even more detailed than the one that sits on the company's intranet:

About 278,000 results

 Ramin Baghai · 2nd
Head of Marketing Global Strategy and Operations at Google
San Francisco Bay Area
👥 Seiji Kawanabe, Delia C. Benitez, and 9 other mutual connections

 Sarah Clark Schiff Hathiramani · 2nd
Director, Product Management, Counter-Abuse Technology at Google
United States
👥 Ganesh Kumar, Bart Rosenthal, and 19 other mutual connections

 Jason Fass · 2nd 🔗
Product Marketing Exec @ Google
Los Gatos, CA
Talks about #leadership, #storytelling, #productmarketing, #fitnesstechnology, and #userexperiencedesign
👥 3K followers · Allen Denison, Steve Sinclair, and 15 other mutual connections

And most importantly, you have a list of hundreds or maybe even thousands of people who could potentially refer you.

But to make sure that they actually want to refer you (i.e., the right-hand side of the Venn diagram), just apply either of these filters:

1) Filter Connections for 1st degree:

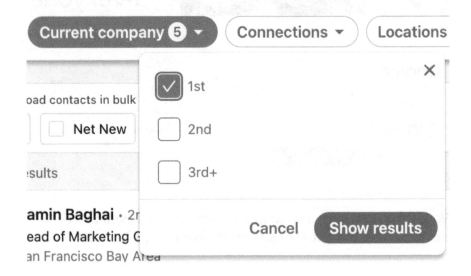

OR

2) Filter School (under All Filter) for every university you've ever attended:

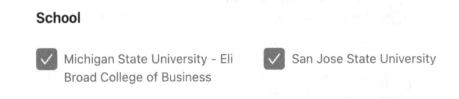

Either way, you now have a list of people who have something in common with you.

So all that's left is to make the ask.

Now, you could spend a lot of time reaching out, setting-up a coffee chat, and going back-and-forth before asking for a referral. And while that might be successful as a long-term investment, the specific job may be long since filled by then.

So I recommend that you just send them an email like the following:

> *Subject: Favor for a fellow Spartan/friend?*
>
> *Hi Elizabeth,*
>
> *May I ask you for a favor (as a fellow Spartan)? I'm really interested in the Associate Product Marketing Manager role at Google as someone with both a deep background in marketing (General Motors) and social impact (Habitat for Humanity).*
>
> *As such, I'm wondering if you'd be open to referring me for the position?*
>
> *If so, here's my resume: LINK. And here's hoping that you get a nice fat referral bonus out of it!*
>
> *Thanks for considering!!!*
> *-John*

No worries if you don't have their email address. You can always look it up in your alumni directory or on www.hunter.io.

And then, to be sure that you maximize your chances, repeat that process with at least 2–3 more employees. That way, if any potential referrer doesn't respond, you still have other irons in the fire.

But why would anyone respond, you might wonder?

The answer lies in two places:

1) The last line of the referral email - because it turns out that most companies will pay a referral bonus whenever an employee refers someone who gets hired. As mentioned earlier, referrals aren't just a source of candidates, but of the very best candidates. So companies tend to reward them with financial incentives that vary from $3,000 (at Khan Academy - which is a nonprofit, by the way!) all the way to $25,000 (at Google - for very in-demand roles).

2) In the referrer's heart - because of a concept called generativity.[3] As selfish as we humans may be sometimes, we also have a bit of an altruistic streak when it comes to the future. And so research has shown that many people have a strong desire to pay it forward to the next generation, even if there's no immediate benefit for them. Hence, reaching out to alumni - even (and especially) those who graduated many years ago - can be an incredibly successful strategy!

But bottom line: The 10X advantage provided by referrals is so crazy powerful that you'd be just-plain crazy not to seek it out!

_____

[3] https://en.wikipedia.org/wiki/Generativity

5) Prepare to Crush Your Interviews

If you've played your AI + human cards right (dozens of personalized applications to a focused set of jobs, supported by a large number of referrals), you should be facing a new challenge now:

"How do I prepare for all these interviews???"

Which is obviously a great problem to have. Especially since it is, like all the problems that have come before it, one that can be tackled through the power of AI!

But before we get into all those ChatGPT interview prep goodies, let's start with the audience we're ultimately trying to impress: *The human being on the other side of the table.*

How Humans Rate Other Humans

Specifically, let's start by understanding how humans evaluate each other.

While many job-seekers tend to think of an interview as just another standardized test to master (a la the SAT or GMAT), nothing could be further from the truth.

That's because decades of research on human perception suggest that, instead of making coldly objective decisions like a Scantron machine (A = Right, B = Wrong), we humans make highly emotional, subjective decisions in the heat of the moment.

Which makes a lot of sense if you think about where we got our start. Imagine one of our predecessors on the Serengeti millennia ago, watching carefully as a fellow Homo sapien approaches. Lacking the ability to look up their LinkedIn profile or do a quick Google search, they have to make a critical decision in the blink of an eye: *Friend or foe?*

And the people who took a long time to think about it?

Well, needless to say, their genes got removed from the pool we all swim in... :)

So here we are 100,000 years later, still making those same, instinctive judgments, albeit in the modern Serengeti - AKA a vast plain of cubicles:

- Can I trust the person on the other side of the table to do a great job?

- And would I even want to do the job with them? Or are they going to stab me in the back someday?

As proof, consider the fact that 33% of interviewers *admit* to making up their minds within **the first 90 seconds of an interview.**[4]

Given that the real proportion is likely much higher, you can see that gut instincts are still the main driver behind human-to-human evaluations.

And what exactly is our gut telling us?

Well, it turns out that reams of sociological research has basically boiled it down to two things:

1. Competence

2. Warmth

---

[4] https://theundercoverrecruiter.com/infographic-how-interviewers-know-when-hire-you-90-seconds/

That's it.

Not "Did they format their interview answers correctly?" or "How strong was their case framework?"

But just:

1. Can they do the job?

2. Do I want to do the job with them?

How to Prep Like a Human

Given this focus on competence and warmth, it's imperative that you prep for your interviews with these as your twin North Stars.

Luckily, there's an easy format that guides you in that direction:

- Challenge
- Action
- Result

While career coaches like to claim they invented this "CAR" format, it's really just the foundation for all great human storytelling.

Take *Star Wars* for example. It's basically a CAR story with nice special effects:

- Challenge: The Death Star is threatening planets around the galaxy
- Action: Luke Skywalker heroically blows up the Death Star
- Result: Peace and prosperity are restored to the galaxy

And the reason we love stories like this is they nail those two qualities we crave:

- **Competence:** A main character capable of doing incredible things

- **Warmth:** The character uses their power for good

So to ensure that your own stories leverage this powerful template, start your prep with this ChatGPT prompt:

> *Generate a list of the 10 most likely interview questions I'll face based on the following job description. And for each question, generate an answer in Challenge - Action - Result format, drawing only from the following resume.*
>
> *Job description: PASTE JOB DESCRIPTION*
>
> *Resume: PASTE RESUME*

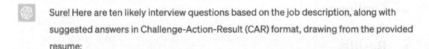 Sure! Here are ten likely interview questions based on the job description, along with suggested answers in Challenge-Action-Result (CAR) format, drawing from the provided resume:

1. Question: Can you provide an example of how you have driven thought leadership and positioned a company in a competitive market to win market share?
   Answer: Challenge: At Fidelis, we faced intense competition in the cybersecurity industry.
   Action: I developed a comprehensive content marketing strategy, creating thought leadership articles, whitepapers, and webinars to showcase our expertise and differentiate us from competitors.
   Result: This approach contributed to a 20% increase in market share within six months and established us as a trusted authority in the industry.

You now have a good template to start practicing with. Just make sure to review each of the stories for accuracy and to add in your own CAR details.

In particular, just like with our Resume Commandments, make sure that each answer is:

- **Concise.** Make your interviewer's life easier by keeping your answer to 1-2 minutes with no insider jargon.

- **Specific.** Instead of just speaking in generalities, call out your precise skills and experiences - i.e., the exact thing that employers crave.

- **Results-oriented.** Prove that you're the obvious choice by demonstrating that you've delivered results before - and you're ready to do so again.

And then, when you're ready to practice, remember that Competence + Warmth really equates to:

- Did the interviewer buy *what* you said?

- Did they like *how* you said it?

So you'll want to make sure you nail the *how* as well as the *what* - which means you also need an AI interview coach.

Luckily, I've got just the "people" for the job:

- ChatGPT

- LinkedIn

ChatGPT is great for practicing your "What." All you need to do is prompt it to play the role of your future interviewer like so:

I want you to interview me for an X ROLE at Y COMPANY. Start by asking me questions based on the job description below. And then, after I answer, please provide constructive criticism on my answer - and ask the next question.

Here is the job description: JOB DESCRIPTION

Next question: How have you developed and executed global demand generation programs in your previous roles?

 When I was at Fidelis, we had very few leads in our CRM. As such, I pioneered a new demand generation program - including our first SDR hire, first automated outreach campaigns, and first nurture experiences. The result was that we generated $40M in new pipeline within just six months.

 Great! It's impressive that you were able to drive such significant results with your demand generation program at Fidelis. Generating $40M in new pipeline within six months is a remarkable achievement.

Constructive criticism: While your answer highlights the outcome of the demand generation program, it would be helpful to provide more specific details about the strategies and tactics you employed to achieve these results. Sharing information about the target audience, channels utilized, and any unique approaches taken would make your answer more comprehensive and impactful.

As you can see, ChatGPT is a safe space to practice responding to new questions and sharing your stories. But it's also an effective space because instead of your standard mock interview where you just go through the motions, you'll now get essential feedback after every answer. Which means that each practice session actually builds your interview muscle! 💪

But don't stop there. Remember that your interviewer will also be influenced by *how* you deliver your answers - not just *what* you say.

So to master your delivery, turn to LinkedIn's free AI-powered Interview Prep tool: linkedin.com/interview-prep

That's right, hidden away in LinkedIn's job board is a full interview coaching system - no Premium account required.

Just pick the most relevant questions for your role (there's both general ones like "Tell me about yourself" and more specific ones like "Tell me about a time you resolved an accounting error") and then do what every top performer does: Record yourself practicing.

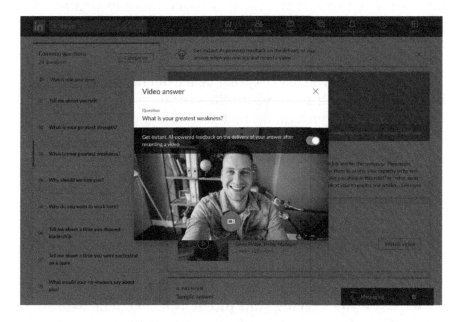

While I know this may feel awkward at first, just know that you're in good company. I mean, can you imagine a star athlete or musician going into the biggest performance of their lives without analyzing and optimizing their recorded practice?

That's because reviewing your practice generates two gifts:

1. It helps you fine-tune the specifics of your delivery (e.g., speaking cadence, dynamic pitch).

2. But it also helps you empathize with the person who's receiving that delivery - i.e., your interviewer.

And as we've stressed throughout this book, the #1 superpower you possess as a job-seeker isn't AI - but your very human ability to empathize with your audience.

So be sure to put yourself in their shoes before you walk into the interview. Chances are, you'll discover a variety of things that *you'll* wish you did, once you see your performance from the *other* side of the interview table!

And not only will you learn a great deal from the practice itself, but LinkedIn's built-in AI coach will give you specific feedback on some of the biggest things that detract from Warmth:

- **Were any of your answers over two minutes?** No one likes a long talker, so make sure to stay concise.

- **Were you talking too quickly or slowly?** Aim for something in the vicinity of 130-160 words per minute, since a slower pace can bore your interviewer and a faster pace can make it hard to keep up.

- **Were you varying your pitch?** The only thing worse than a long answer is a long answer that all... sounds... the... same. So be sure to spice up your response with occasional highs and lows.

- **Did you fall back on any filler words ("um," "like," etc.)?** No one wants to work with a Valley Girl/Surfer Dude, so be careful... ;)

Plus, if you want to really step up your interview game, remember that a great job search is a specific job search - i.e., one that's tailored to precise roles and companies, not just generic desperation!

So in the context of your interview preparation, that means getting feedback that's specific to a company. Especially since every company prioritizes different values and skillsets.

And thus, the virtue of doing this interview prep on LinkedIn is that, once your AI coach has had a chance to weigh in, you can also share your answers with people in your network *inside* the company. Which should be a piece of cake, given that you've been connecting with insiders since our very first step.

So go ahead and request feedback from the folks you've met to make sure you're fully ready for primetime:

Request feedback   ✕

Search connections

Your connections
Recommended by job title

Clint Korver
Managing Director at Ulu Ventures

Meg Garlinghouse
Connecting talent to opportunity at massive scale to impact the world

Dan Reardon
Growth Marketing VP/Senior Director | Performance Marketing Leader, E-commerce Expertise, International Expansion | Leading Growth Marketing for late-stage start ups or public B2C companies

And then, the night before the Big Interview, I recommend trying two more ChatGPT prompts to get you in the right mindset:

1) What are the 5 biggest challenges and opportunities facing X COMPANY?

2) What's a 90-day action plan to tackle the job described in this job description: PASTE JOB DESCRIPTION

A 90-day action plan to tackle the Chief Marketing Officer (CMO) job described in the job description would involve the following steps:

1. Understand the Company and Market Landscape:

- Familiarize yourself with the company's products, target audience, industry positioning, and competition.
- Review the current marketing strategies, initiatives, and key performance indicators (KPIs).
- Conduct a comprehensive market analysis to identify industry trends, customer needs, and potential opportunities.

Because the real idea behind Competence + Warmth is that your interviewer is trying to predict the future: Are you friend or foe? Awesome colleague or disastrous hire?

And so the more you can start to envision helping the company solve its challenges, take advantage of its opportunities, and get the job done, the more you can paint a positive picture of the future for your interviewer.

So leverage the power of AI one last time - and then get ready to apply all those computer-generated insights to master the most important algorithm of all: *Human decision-making!*

6) Negotiate Like a Robot

By this chapter, I trust that congrats are in order.

You've found the perfect path, gotten recruiters to compete for your talent, and have at least one job offer in hand.

But resist the temptation to just sign that offer and be done with it.

Instead, recognize that the incredible investment you've made in this process deserves an incredible payoff. And the only way to ensure that all your hard work is rewarded is to:

1. Make sure you choose the best role for *you*

2. Make sure you get the best offer for *your market*

I'll show you exactly how to optimize both outcomes in the next two sections.

Keep Your Eyes on the Prize

The first big mistake that job-seekers make with negotiation is that they focus primarily on compensation. While prioritizing salary may seem logical ("I just put in all this work - I'm ready to get paid!"), come back to the first principles we established at the start of the book: A *great* job search is a *focused* job search.

As we discussed, being focused not only helps recruiters find you, it helps you land the job that's right for you; the job that fits *your* unique interests and skills - not just the one that looks good to your friends or family!

And while we leveraged ChatGPT and LinkedIn in that early chapter to hone in on the right focus, we, admittedly, were operating at a fairly high level - e.g., here are some generally good job titles, not specific job opportunities.

Whereas now, at the end of your search, you have so much more specific information to go on. You know the kinds of projects you'd work on, the kinds of people you'd work with, and the kinds of goals you'd work towards.

So before you even begin to ponder compensation, it makes sense to come back to ChatGPT with that more specific context:

My career goal is X, my skills are Y, and my interests are Z. Based on this context, please evaluate the following job opportunities to help me determine which is the best fit:

INSERT OFFERS

 My career goal is to become a CEO, my skills are in analytics and public speaking, and my interests are focused on education and the environment. Based on this context, please evaluate the following job opportunities to help me determine which is the best fit:

-Product Manager, Google Maps
-Program Manager, Tesla
-Product Marketing Manager, Apple Watch

 Sure, let's take a look at each of these roles and how they align with your skills, interests, and career goals.

1. **Product Manager, Google Maps**: As a Product Manager, you would have the opportunity to utilize your analytical skills to make data-driven decisions about the product's direction. You would also employ your public speaking skills during presentations to stakeholders. Google is known for its environmental initiatives, so this role might align with your interest in the environment. However, it might not directly relate to your interest in education. If your goal is to become a CEO, a product manager role could be a good stepping stone as it involves managing a product's lifecycle, which could provide you with leadership experience and business acumen.

But let's be real: As great as any job looks on paper, at the end of the day, so much of your success and satisfaction will come down to the one person who's not on that piece of paper... i.e., your boss.

Don't believe me? Just ask the 75% of all recently-departed employees who told Gallup their bosses were the primary reason for their departure:

So what's a prospective employee to do?

After all, it seems like the bosses have all the power. They get to put you through the hiring gauntlet:

- Resume
- Cover letter
- LinkedIn profile
- Take-home project
- Phone screens
- In-person interviews
- Background checks

Whereas you seemingly just have a single choice: Take the offer or leave it.

At least, that's the way things *used* to work.

But remember, we're living in the age of LinkedIn, which means you now get to do your *own* background check - on your prospective boss.

Here's how:

1. **Set your background check target.** As convenient as it would be to just ask current employees, let's be honest: Even disgruntled employees can be loath to share their true feelings with outsiders - it just seems to violate some unspoken insider circle of trust. Whereas people who've left the company are no longer obligated to conceal the truth - be it due to health insurance, stock options, or pure loyalty.

2. **Find former employees on LinkedIn.** While running a People Search, just click "All Filters" and then select your prospective employer from the "Past Company" list.

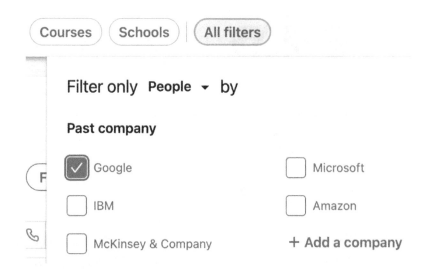

3. **Filter for people from your prospective team.** While any former employee might be able to give you a taste for the overall company culture, what you really need is insight about your specific prospective boss. So be sure to filter for that (e.g., Product Manager, Google Maps) in the Search box at top.

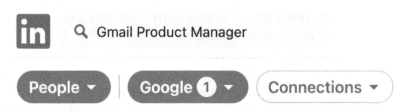

4. **Filter for people with something in common.** While it might be tempting just to reach out to these former insiders, ideally you'll have even more connective tissue to earn their trust and transparency. So try filtering for people who know your friends (2nd Degree Connections) or people who went to your same school.

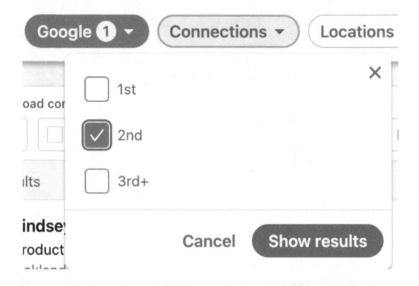

5. **Reach out the right way.** Once you've identified former insiders with something in common, send them a Connection Request on LinkedIn like this:

   "Did you work with X BOSS at Y COMPANY by any chance? If so, I'd love to know if you'd recommend taking a role on their team since I've just gotten an offer from them. Very cool to see that we both KNOW X MUTUAL CONTACT/ WENT TO Y SCHOOL!"

   Note that this approach both keeps it simple (since, as mentioned before, we always want to make it easy for them to respond) and adds in the additional layer of social connection (to earn their trust).

6. **Compile your feedback.** Lastly, just like we didn't want to choose a path based purely on one person's opinion, we don't want to overindex our choice of bosses based on one former employee. So try to reach out to at least five former colleagues in the hopes of getting 3+ points of feedback. And then let the ratio of positive:negative comments guide your ultimate decision.

With your ideal offer starting to become clearer, it's time to make sure that the quality of the opportunity is matched by the quality of the contract.

How Recruiters Are Incentivized

Just like a prized painting would never be sold outside an open auction, don't just sell your talent based on the first bid - instead, hold out for the *best* bid.

And that means creating your own auction of sorts - via the power of negotiation!

Just like any successful auction, three things are critical here:

1. Have as many bidders as possible

2. Make the bidders as aware of each other as possible

3. Understand the bidders' motivations

We'll come back to #1 and #2 in the next section. But for now, let's focus on #3: Understanding your bidders' - AKA your recruiters' - motivations.

Because contrary to the image that recruiters project ("Take it or leave it - this is our only offer"), they're actually in a precarious position.

Specifically, all the power they enjoyed at the start of the process has now swung to you!

Why?

For the simple reason that hiring is all a numbers game. At the beginning of your search, the numbers favored your dream role.

After all, there was only one amazing job - but hundreds or maybe thousands of talented applicants.

But now, at the final stage, there's only you - the dream candidate. And there are potentially multiple suitors competing for your talents.

In other words: *Advantage you.*

To understand what's behind this leverage, imagine how devastating it would feel for a recruiter, who's worked so hard to reel in the best talent, to now have to start from scratch.

Nothing could be worse for *them*. Which is why everything is perfect for *you*.

That is, *if* you negotiate, of course... So let's talk exactly about how to do that the right way.

How to Negotiate

Now that we know exactly how recruiters approach the negotiation, let's tackle the two other key factors:

1. Having as many bidders as possible

2. Making the bidders as aware of each other as possible

Just like a competitive auction depends upon multiple bidders, you want to get as many suitors competing for your talents as possible.

To do so, the first rule is to stay in as many talent pools for *as long as you can*. So don't make the rookie mistake of bowing out of the hiring process early for jobs you're not thrilled about.

Instead, even if a role doesn't seem perfect, keep on pushing to see how far you can make it.

That way, when it comes time to negotiate for the role you genuinely do want, you can credibly point to a variety of employers competing for you.

Which leads to our second rule: A potential competitor only matters *if your recruiter knows about them*. So don't make the other big rookie mistake of collecting lots of interviews and offers - but keeping them all in the dark about each other.

Instead, let the light shine by generating a polite but powerful message to the recruiter using this prompt:

> *Generate a short, conversational email to the recruiter at X COMPANY, letting them know about my other interviews/offers at Y COMPANY and Z COMPANY. Ask them if, in light of these competitive opportunities, they can do ABC (accelerate their interview process, make a final decision sooner, or offer a more competitive package).*

Generate a short, conversational email to the recruiter at Google, letting them know about my other interviews at Facebook and Apple. Ask them if, in light of these competitive opportunities, they can accelerate their interview process.

 Subject: Exciting Opportunities at Facebook and Apple - Request for Accelerated Interview Process

Dear [Recruiter's Name],

I hope this email finds you well. I wanted to reach out and provide you with an update on my job search progress. I'm excited to share that I have interviews scheduled with Facebook and Apple, two incredible companies in the tech industry.

Considering the competitive nature of these opportunities and my strong interest in joining Google, I was wondering if it would be possible to accelerate the interview process. I truly believe that Google is the ideal organization for me to grow both personally and professionally, and I would be thrilled to have the chance to contribute to its innovative culture.

No matter where you are in the process (from getting close to an offer to having a less-than-perfect offer in-hand), this shot across the bow will put the recruiter on notice that your particular talent auction will be a competitive one.

Why does this strategy work so well?

Because there's something deeply human and painful about losing out to the competition. Just like FOMO gnaws at us when we look through our friends' Instagrams, feeling like we're about to miss out on the perfect candidate - and to our bitter rival, no less - stirs up a potent mix of anticipated regret and a hunger to fight.

Which is why even the most desirable employers aren't immune to this approach. After all, at the end of the day, even the Googles and Disneys of the world are run by people. And as I shared in my own example, even the Google recruiter couldn't resist fighting for my talent when he felt threatened by a competitive offer.

That said, this is only the first step in the delicate dance that is negotiation.

So once you've established your competitive positioning, it's time to take the next step: Setting a favorable anchor.

Just like a ship's anchor keeps it within a tight radius of where it's docked, a negotiating anchor establishes a clear band for the conversation.

And while the employer technically gets to establish the first anchor when they send you an offer, there's no reason to be wed to that - especially if it undervalues your talent.

Which brings up an important question: How *do* you actually value your talent?

Since value is, as they say, in the eye of the beholder, it's critical to start by finding the best possible beholder... :)

And that means shopping across a variety of comparisons to find the most favorable one, including:

- How much you're making in your current job

- How much other employers are offering you

- How much similar roles are paid in your location

So, in addition to #1 and #2, be sure to check out Glassdoor and Payscale to get a sense of #3.

Note: While it may be tempting to leverage ChatGPT here, the fact that so much of its training data comes from 2021 and before makes it less reliable for generating up-to-date comparables.

And then, when you find the best possible comparison, it's time to make that the new anchor for the negotiation. Especially since it's a lot easier to offer a little wiggle room from a high point than to try to nudge an employer up from a low position.

To establish this new anchor, recognize that negotiation is almost always easier to do over email. That way, you have a chance to sit back and review all your options vs. accepting something rashly in the heat of a live conversation.

So come back to ChatGPT with a prompt like this:

> *Generate a short, conversational email to my recruiter, thanking them for their kind job offer (INSERT OFFER), and letting them know that I'd like to explore what's possible based on the following facts:*
>
> *-Current Salary*
>
> *-Other Offers*
>
> *-Pay Research for Role/Location*

Generate a short, conversational email to my recruiter, thanking them for their kind job offer ($100K), and letting them know that I'd like to explore what's possible based on the following facts:
-Current Salary: ($105K)
-Other Offers: Facebook offered me $110K
-Pay Research for Role/Location: The average PM makes $115K in Denver

Subject: Gratitude for the Job Offer and Consideration for Salary Discussion

Dear [Recruiter's Name],

I hope this email finds you well. I wanted to take a moment to express my sincere gratitude for the job offer you extended to me. I'm thrilled about the opportunity to join your esteemed company and contribute to its success.

Before we move forward, I would like to explore what is possible regarding the compensation package. I understand that you offered a salary of $100,000, which I truly appreciate. However, I would like to provide some additional information for your consideration:

1. Current Salary: Currently, my salary at my current position stands at $105,000. While compensation is not the sole determining factor, I believe it's important to ensure a fair transition and recognize the value I bring to the table.

What you'll get back will likely be more tactful and clear than what we could compose on our own, given that ChatGPT removes all the emotion and ego from the negotiation - and keeps things focused on the facts. Which, not incidentally, favor you! :)

At this point, you may get a variety of responses ranging from a "We don't negotiate" to a "We'll get back to you" to a new, compromise offer.

No matter what you get, I highly recommend just feeding it right back to ChatGPT:

> *I asked my recruiter to match this offer: X. They came back with the following message: Y. Generate a short, conversational response that asks them to do better, given my opportunities at these other firms: Z*

I asked my recruiter to match this offer: $110K. They came back with the following message: "The best we can do is $105K". Generate a short, conversational response that asks them to do better, given my opportunities at these other firms: Facebook.

 Hey [Recruiter's Name],

Thanks for getting back to me. I appreciate your efforts in considering my request. However, considering the opportunities I have at other firms like Facebook, I was hoping we could come closer to the $110K offer. Is there any room for further negotiation? I believe my skills and experience make me a valuable asset, and I'm really excited about the potential to contribute to your team.

Looking forward to hearing your thoughts.

Best regards,
[Your Name]

Because, again, while we have a human temptation to just fold at the first sign of resistance, remember that:

- The recruiters are way more desperate than you at this stage

- ChatGPT can take the fear and anxiety out of your side - and amp it up on their side

That said, at some point of this back-and-forth, you may get to a genuine impasse. That's because many companies have fixed salary bands (e.g., we can pay Product Managers anywhere from $90–110K) - which gives recruiters wiggle room within them but not the authority to exceed them.

So if a recruiter can't match your salary comparison, consider whether there are other things you can ask for instead, including:

- Sign-on bonus
- Equity

- Relocation package
- Better title
- Remote work flexibility
- More vacation time
- Earlier or later start
- Or whatever else is most important to you

That's because while salaries tend to be the most tightly banded part of an offer, recruiters and teams generally have more flexibility with all of the above.

So if you're willing to get creative, try a prompt like this to keep things moving when you're feeling stuck:

> *Generate a short, conversational email to my recruiter offering a concession of X salary in exchange for Y benefit.*

 Generate a short, conversational email to my recruiter offering a concession of $5K in salary in exchange for 5 more vacation days.

 Hey [Recruiter's Name],

I hope you're doing well. After giving it some thought, I wanted to propose a potential adjustment to the offer we discussed. Instead of the original salary of $110K, I'm willing to accept a concession of $5K, which would bring the salary down to $105K. In exchange, I would love to have an additional five vacation days per year. I believe this would strike a good balance between compensation and personal time, allowing me to bring my best to the team while still taking care of my well-being.

Let me know what you think about this suggestion. I'm eager to find a solution that works well for both of us.

Thanks,
[Your Name]

And then, if you're still stuck after exhausting all other options, don't hesitate to offer your recruiter a helping hand.

"A helping hand???," you say. "Why would I do that after this whole back-and-forth?"

Because remember that you hold the upper hand: Control over the scarcest resource - AKA your talent.

And so letting a recruiter know that you're *this* close to signing with them is **SO** tempting.

Thus, whenever you're ready to settle the offer for good, just employ a prompt like this:

> *Generate a short, conversational email to my recruiter letting them know that I'm willing to consider signing their offer today and turning down my other offers - but only if they can agree to X compensation now.*

 Generate a short, conversational email to my recruiter letting them know that I'm willing to consider signing their offer today and turning down my other offers - but only if they can agree to a $5K sign-on bonus now.

 Hey [Recruiter's Name],

I hope this email finds you well. I wanted to express my genuine excitement about the prospect of joining your team. After careful consideration, I am strongly leaning towards accepting your offer and turning down my other options.

However, before I make a final decision, I was wondering if there might be room to discuss a $5K sign-on bonus. If we could reach an agreement on this now, it would greatly influence my choice and provide a strong incentive for me to commit fully to your organization.

If it's possible to include the sign-on bonus in the offer today, I am more than willing to sign and accept the position. I believe that my skills and expertise would be a valuable addition to your team, and I am eager to contribute to the company's success.

Thank you for your understanding and consideration. I look forward to hearing your response and hopefully reaching a mutually beneficial agreement.

The result will be such manna from heaven to any recruiter, that it's almost certain to squeeze out that last final concession.

And now, after your long, epic journey, through AI, LinkedIn, and the wilds of the hiring landscape, you can rest easy knowing that you made it to the promised land. And you did it the absolute best way - the way that's true to you.

Conclusion: Search Like a Robot, Succeed Like a Human

As tempting as it might be to just wrap up here, I want to put our journey together into a slightly broader context to really turbocharge your efforts.

So let's start with the surprising finding from a recent survey: What % of employees do you think said they'd be willing to give up $5,000 to be happier at work?

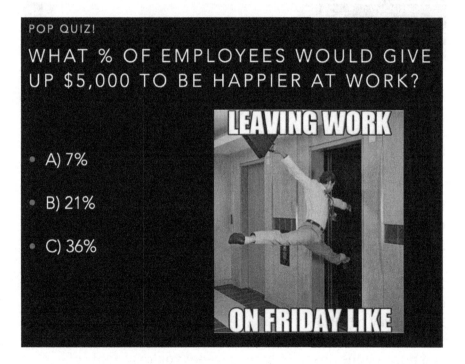

Was it roughly 1 in 10, 2 in 10, or more than 3 in 10?

Well, if you guessed 36%, you're absolutely right.

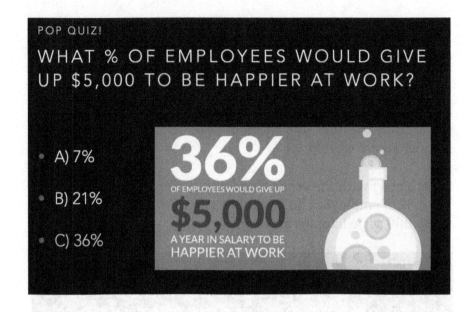

WHAT % OF EMPLOYEES WOULD GIVE UP $5,000 TO BE HAPPIER AT WORK?

- A) 7%

- B) 21%

- C) 36%

36%
OF EMPLOYEES WOULD GIVE UP
$5,000
A YEAR IN SALARY TO BE
HAPPIER AT WORK

But the real question is: "Why?"

After all, isn't the point of work to make money? You know, to buy us food, shelter, clothing - all the basics. And so why would anyone want to make less money at work?

Well, as you've probably figured out by now, just like there's way more to resumes than random bullet points, there's way more to work than just paying the bills.

Because as the famous psychologist, Abraham Maslow, figured out almost 100 years ago, we've also got deeply human needs that go way beyond survival. Things like building strong bonds with other people, being recognized for what you're great at, and pushing the absolute limits of what you're capable of.

And wouldn't you know it, but work - or at least great work - can be an incredible path to all of those things. Whether it's being part of something bigger than yourself, showcasing your strengths, or doing something no one ever thought possible, a great job is not just a way of paying the bills. **It's a way of building a life you love.**

And as artificial and painful as the hiring process can feel sometimes, it's the gateway to that great job and the life that comes with it. So as you invest time and energy in traversing this path, don't ever forget why you're working so hard:

Not to make a recruiter's life easier, or your own life easier - but to give your future self what you deserve: *A career - and a life - well-lived.*

So here's wishing you good luck on all your endeavors. And please, please, please do me one huge favor: Let me know where your next adventure takes you.

The greatest gift for a career coach is hearing about what people are capable of when they can access the opportunities they dream of. So hopefully I've inspired you to dream big - and I'd love to be inspired by your journey in return! 🙏

Get a Cutting-Edge Bonus

Thanks so much for reading!

As you can probably tell by now, I'm a pretty big geek... 🤓

So I've cooked up one extra special bonus just for superstar job-seekers: **CareerCoachBot**

Here's how it works:

1. Review this book on your favorite site.

2. Once your review goes live, share it at bit.ly/careercoachbot

That's it!

Instead of manually entering prompts into ChatGPT one-by-one, all you need to do is enter your interests and resume into my tool and you'll get immediate coaching on the perfect path + application process.

Rock on! 🤘

About the Author

Jeremy Schifeling has devoted his career to helping others succeed in theirs.

From teaching kindergarten in Brooklyn to recruiting top students at Teach For America to leading education marketing at LinkedIn, he's touched the lives of millions of people at every stage of their journeys.

Along the way, he's published the best-selling LinkedIn book on Amazon, served as a career coach for military veterans at Shift.org and MBA students at the University of Michigan, and produced the most-viewed video in LinkedIn's history.

He currently leads marketing at Khan Academy and shares his thoughts on thejobinsiders.com, a site for anyone who wants to build a better career - and life!

Made in the USA
Monee, IL
09 February 2024

53170880R00098